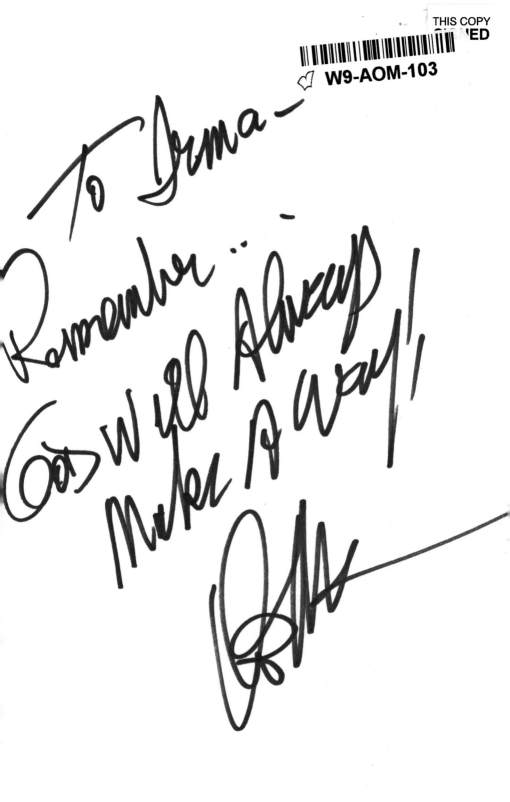

To Irma —

Remember ...

God Will Always

Make A Way!

# PRAISE FOR
## *GOD WILL MAKE A WAY*

"A person would need to look a long time to find a purer heart and voice than those of Don Moen. I'm honored to call him a friend and thrilled at the release of his book."

—MAX LUCADO, PASTOR AND BESTSELLING AUTHOR

"Don Moen has been a personal presence in my life for almost three decades. His influence and the example his family has been to mine is incalculable. Now, with his new book *God Will Make a Way*, Don has delivered one of the major components of why he was placed on this earth. This is the book we have been waiting for!"

—ANDY ANDREWS, *NEW YORK TIMES*
BESTSELLING AUTHOR OF *THE TRAVELER'S*
*GIFT* AND *THE NOTICER*

"Don Moen is my friend and has been for a long time. I've seen him win awards and be celebrated. I've seen him in the depths of despair, wondering if God was near. In each situation, he emerged on the other side, fully God's man. This book tells you how he does it."

—STEPHEN MANSFIELD, *NEW YORK TIMES*
BESTSELLING AUTHOR AND
INTERNATIONAL SPEAKER

"It's incredibly difficult at times to see how your most difficult challenges can become your greatest breakthroughs. As we read *God Will Make a Way*, we were truly impacted. Don shares from his own deeply personal experiences, life-changing stories, spiritual truths, and godly wisdom that will ignite your faith, refocus your perspective, and give you the impetus to overcome and thrive through whatever challenge you may be facing."

—ALVIN AND JOY SLAUGHTER, ALVIN AND
JOY SLAUGHTER INTERNATIONAL

"Don Moen has been a close friend for more than twenty-five years. I have watched him minister to a small room of believers and then stand on a stage in front of hundreds of thousands of people all over the world, and he is always the same man on or off the stage. Drawing from timeless Scripture and experiences in Don's life, *God Will Make a Way* confronts us with the reality of a powerful, personal God who is prepared to make a way for each of us, even in the most difficult circumstances."

—PAUL BALOCHE, SONGWRITER AND WORSHIP LEADER

*God Will Make a Way*

# God Will Make a Way

*Discovering His Hope in Your Story*

# DON MOEN

WITH ROBERT NOLAND

## EMANATE
BOOKS

Published in Nashville, Tennessee, by Emanate Books, an imprint of Thomas Nelson. Emanate Books and Thomas Nelson are registered trademarks of HarperCollins Christian Publishing, Inc.

Published in association of the literary agency Iconic Media Brands LLC.

Thomas Nelson titles may be purchased in bulk for educational, business, fund-raising, or sales promotional use. For information, please e-mail SpecialMarkets@ThomasNelson.com.

Unless otherwise noted, Scripture quotations are taken from the New King James Version®. © 1982 by Thomas Nelson. Used by permission. All rights reserved.

Scripture quotations marked GW are from God's Word®. Copyright © 1995 God's Word to the Nations. Used by permission of Baker Publishing Group. All rights reserved.

Scripture quotations marked THE MESSAGE are from The Message. Copyright © by Eugene H. Peterson 1993, 1994, 1995, 1996, 2000, 2001, 2002. Used by permission of NavPress. All rights reserved. Represented by Tyndale House Publishers, Inc.

Scripture quotations marked NASB are from New American Standard Bible®. Copyright © 1960, 1962, 1963, 1968, 1971, 1972, 1973, 1975, 1977, 1995 by The Lockman Foundation. Used by permission. (www.Lockman.org)

Scripture quotations marked NIV are from the Holy Bible, New International Version®, NIV®. Copyright © 1973, 1978, 1984, 2011 by Biblica, Inc.® Used by permission of Zondervan. All rights reserved worldwide. www.Zondervan.com. The "NIV" and "New International Version" are trademarks registered in the United States Patent and Trademark Office by Biblica, Inc.®

Scripture quotations marked NLT are from the Holy Bible, New Living Translation. © 1996, 2004, 2007, 2013, 2015 by Tyndale House Foundation. Used by permission of Tyndale House Publishers, Inc., Carol Stream, Illinois 60188. All rights reserved.

Scripture quotations marked WEB are from the World English Bible™. Public domain.

ISBN 978-0-7852-2257-6 (eBook)
ISBN 978-0-7852-2220-0 (HC)
ISBN 978-0-7852-2895-0 (IE)

**Library of Congress Control Number: 2018943315**

*Printed in the United States of America*
18  19  20  21  22    LSC    10  9  8  7  6  5  4  3  2  1

To Craig and Susan Phelps:
Your lives are a living example of how God is able to make a
way where there seems to be no way. Your story of trusting
God through your personal loss continues to bring hope to
those who have lost hope.


To Jeremy Jacob Phelps:
Born September 2, 1978, graduated to heaven March 18, 1987.

"Since you were precious in My sight,
You have been honored,
And I have loved you;
Therefore I will give men for you,
And people for your life."
(Isaiah 43:4)

# CONTENTS

# FOREWORD

Don Moen is a friend of mine, and as someone who has been touched not only by his ministry but also by his friendship, I can tell you that the man you see on stage is the same man you meet in private. He loves his family, he loves his friends, and above all he loves the Lord.

One of my favorite Don Moen songs is "God Will Make a Way." As I look back on my childhood, I can remember the days we didn't have food. I can recall the nights we slept in a cardboard box and had no home. I still haven't forgotten my first pair of shoes I received at age twelve. Those were difficult times. Today I look back and am thankful for those experiences. I am thankful because I now know that God was making a way for me even before I could see it.

I know what it's like to be hungry, I know what it's like to be worried about the future. Maybe you are facing a future that has you scared. Maybe you're not sure what to do next. I want you to know that in the middle of your troubles and your sorrow and your fear God is there. He is there with you just like He was there with me on the streets selling flowers to buy food and in the cardboard box as I slept without a home. He is with you today.

Don Moen believes the same thing about God. No matter how bad things may look, you must believe that God will somehow make a way for you. That's why I like this new book so much, just the title gives you hope—*God Will Make a Way*. Yes, I believe that. Because I believe that, I try to help other people see that God is there for them.

This is the message of the book, and I know you will be very encouraged by it. We will all face tough times, but how will we respond when life knocks us down? I can tell you from my time in the ring, you have to get up. You have to. You must believe that even though hard times have come your way that God is still good and that all things are still possible when you turn to Him. Like the boxing coach in the corner during a prize fight, you must listen to God because He can see the battle from a different point of view. And He wants you to win.

When you read *God Will Make a Way*, I believe you will see how God has helped many other people and how much God wants to help you too.

Emmanuel "Manny" D. Pacquiao

General Santos City, Philippines

# A PERSONAL NOTE TO THE
# WEARY AND THE LEARY

*I can't. . . . I just can't do this any longer.*

*I don't think I will ever be able to overcome this. It's just too much.*

*I don't think that will ever happen for me. I used to believe, but I
don't anymore.*

*What good does it do to keep believing in something that will
never come?*

*I don't know what I'm going to do. I have no idea where to turn now.*

*I should just make things easier on everyone and give up.*

Do you relate to any of these statements? Are your life circumstances
summed up in one or more of these sentences? Are any of these words
your true expressions from deep within your own heart, whether you
have spoken them out loud or not? Or maybe you've said them and are
now trying to crawl out from under the crushing weight and reality of
those devastating thoughts and feelings.

We all use the words *can't, won't, don't,* and *hasn't* far too often these days in our downward-spiraling and broken world. The word at the end of each of these contractions is *not*. That little three-letter word is quite powerful to be able to turn any positive into a negative. Can*not* happen. Will *not* happen. Does *not* happen. Has *not* happened.

When we are right in the midst of a life crisis or staring at one headed straight for us, we can drive past the many church marquees, read their short cliché messages, and wonder, *Who gets to actually live the blissful lives those words are talking about?*

"God is good all the time."

"God will make a way."

"All things are possible if you only believe."

In the stark reality of our circumstances, faith statements like these can feel like they are mocking us, condemning our circumstances. Sure, we want the words to be true. Oh, how we want them to be true! But on our deepest, darkest, most desperate days, we decide to place the *not* beside any thought that might tease us with false hope. *Can't. Won't. Don't.* Case closed.

But the reality of our lives is that when our plans are working on all cylinders and the sky in our world is a blissful and beautiful blue, when the bank account is blessed and the pantry full, when our health is good and our relationships connecting, we tend to think that and act like we don't need God and His simple messages of faith and hope. All is well, thank you very much. But when the storm clouds gather and the bottom drops out of life, that is when we reach up and out, grasping for His help, even if we tell no one that we did.

Trials can change both our context of life and our perspective of God. All too often, experiencing struggles is the only way that will happen. The *can't, won't, don't* life creeps in and cries out for something far bigger than our weakness and creates a desperation for answers beyond what we can possibly provide on our own.

The very real story of what quite unintentionally became the signature song of my music career, "God Will Make a Way," was born out of a tragedy that started me on the path to understanding that when storms threaten our lives, we are about to see the power of God move in miraculous ways. Here's the catch though. We must make the intentional decision to look for Him there. He *will* make a way, but will we see it? Our sinful, selfish DNA is wired to miss Him and only sink deeper into our *can't, won't, don't* lives.

Deciding to look for God in our storms instead of staring helplessly at the wind and waves can bring simple truths like a church marquee message, an encouraging word from a friend, or the words of a book to offer authentic hope that can cut through the darkest nights, the most tragic circumstances.

Jesus said that He didn't come for the healthy but for the sick (Matt. 9:12). I didn't write my song, the simple melodic message God has used to touch thousands upon thousands of people all around the world, for those who live lives untouched and unaffected up on the mountain, but rather for those who find themselves alone and hurting in the valley—even those who can't find the strength or the will to live another day. Likewise, I believe the message found in these pages will resonate with those ready for real heavenly hope.

I have no idea what your situation may be. Maybe you have been walking with Christ for years and this book will become one of the many you have read to spur you on in your faith. Or maybe someone gave you this book because of a struggle you are facing and right about now you are questioning whether you will even turn to the next page. You're looking for a reason to put this book down and not pick it back up.

Regardless of your circumstances or station in life, whether you have experienced God making a way for you countless times or you have real doubts if there is a God at all who can make *any* way, much less one for you, I want to encourage you to dig in and read these stories that I have lived, witnessed, and experienced. My prayer is that you find *your own life* here, that you will turn to a new chapter and a fresh start, no matter your situation.

Maybe, just maybe, you will find out for yourself that there is indeed a God who can and will make a way . . . *for you*. In fact, I'm willing to guarantee you that, if you are open, He will speak to you and show you exactly who He is by the end of this book. If He really is God, then why couldn't He do that? Why wouldn't He do that for you?

How could I possibly make such a guarantee and raise such questions?

While I am best known for my music, here's the irony in my résumé. If you put a bunch of singers in a room, I won't be the best vocalist there. If you line up piano players, I won't win the keyboard competition. But that's because for decades I have served a God who chooses the weak, considers the foolish, and counts those who don't believe they count. And if He did that for Don Moen, He will do it for you. To be honest, that is the only reason I am writing this book—because I truly believe that God will make a way in your life just as He has in mine.

As we move forward together, I want to help you remove some of the *not*s in the *can't, won't, don't* life—to believe that what has been consuming you in this season can change to a very different message, one of hope and grace. And by the time you finish this book, I pray that you will be able to remove the *not*s and turn all the opening statements in this introduction around to make new and hopeful declarations for your life.

*I can. . . . I can do this.*
*I will be able to overcome this.*
*I believe that will happen for me. I do.*
*Why would I dare stop believing for something that can most*
  *certainly come?*
*I think I know what I'm going to do. I know where to turn now.*
*I should make things easier on myself and give it to God.*

But he said to me, "My grace is sufficient for you, for my power is made perfect in weakness." Therefore I will boast all the more gladly about my weaknesses, so that Christ's power may rest on me. That is why, for Christ's sake, I delight in weaknesses, in insults, in hardships, in persecutions, in difficulties. For when I am weak, then I am strong. (2 Cor. 12:9–10 NIV)

# chapter one

# THROUGH THE STORM

Late one night our phone rang. One of those calls that is unexpected enough that the likely chance of bad news flashes across your mind. I answered to hear the voice of my mother-in-law and immediately knew something was very wrong.

My wife's sister and her family had been traveling from Oklahoma to Colorado for a ski vacation. On a lonely stretch of highway at an intersection, their van was broadsided by an eighteen-wheeler. Three of Susan and Craig Phelps's sons were seriously injured. But when Craig got to Jeremy, their oldest, he quickly realized his body was already lifeless.

In a heartbeat, their beloved firstborn was taken from them.

Literally within seconds, a happy, close-knit family on their way to a week of fun and relaxation in the mountains was thrown into a sea of suffering and life would never be the same again.

You can never be prepared for those moments. They suck the life out of you like a sudden punch to the gut and it can take years to feel like you can even breathe again. Every day becomes an effort to not drown in your own sorrow.

My immediate response upon hearing the news was to want to do something—*anything*. But in all my days, I had never felt so helpless. Our dearly loved family members were alone, hundreds of miles away in another state, suddenly thrust into and enduring an agony beyond anything we could imagine.

All the scriptures I knew about hurt and loss flew up from my heart into my mind, but they all somehow seemed to fall short of what I really wanted to convey to Susan and Craig. Even for committed Christians, very true and well-intended Bible verses quoted at a misguided time can end up feeling like religious daggers to the heart, like standards that in the darkest of moments we can't possibly meet. Our pain is just too present.

The truth was I didn't know what to say. The reality was I didn't have any answers to give. I had to face the fact that I couldn't, no matter how badly I wanted to, ease their aching hearts. There was no possible human way to *fix* this.

## Roadways and Rivers

The next day while on the plane, I kept asking God to give me a word of encouragement for the family. I opened my Bible and began reading from Isaiah 43:

> "Fear not, for I have redeemed you;
> I have called you by your name;
> You are Mine.
> When you pass through the waters, I will be with you;
> And through the rivers, they shall not overflow you.

When you walk through the fire, you shall not be burned,

Nor shall the flame scorch you.

For I am the LORD your God,

The Holy One of Israel, your Savior. . . .

Since you were precious in My sight,

You have been honored,

And I have loved you;

Therefore I will give men for you,

And people for your life."

(vv. 1–4)

As I read further in the chapter, verses 18 and 19 jumped off the page and grabbed me by the heart.

"Do not call to mind the former things,

Or ponder things of the past.

"Behold, I will do something new,

Now it will spring forth;

Will you not be aware of it?

I will even make a roadway in the wilderness,

Rivers in the desert." (NASB)

*Wilderness* and *desert* were exactly the right descriptors for this horrible place into which our family had been thrown without warning. But God was saying He would meet us there, that He is the God of the wilderness and the desert as much as God of the road and the river.

Traveling at thirty thousand feet between heaven and earth, I eased back in my seat, closed my eyes, and began to intercede for Susan, Craig, and their three boys in the hospital, whispering words I will never

3

forget: "Lord, please make a road in the wilderness and create rivers in the desert for this family today." I knew they were all trapped in a rising flood of grief, pain, and the horrible what-ifs overwhelming them, as well as walking through a fire that seemed to be all-consuming.

As I kept praying those words from Isaiah over and over on their behalf, a simple melody and lyric began to rise up from my spirit, and as was my usual response, I began to sketch the words and notes out on a legal pad as quickly as they were given to me.

> *By a roadway in the wilderness, He'll lead me*
> *Rivers in the desert will I see*
> *Heaven and earth will fade but His Word will still remain*
> *He will do something new today*
> *God will make a way where there seems to be no way*
> *He works in ways we cannot see*
> *He will make a way for me*
> *He will be my guide, hold me closely to His side*
> *With love and strength for each new day*
> *He will make a way*
> *He will make a way*[1]

Looking at the words on the pad, I knew God had given me this song to share with Craig and Susan, not for an audience of thousands but for just two, flowing out from the words of His timeless prophet, hope spoken into a hopeless situation, encouragement delivered into the fury of fear. I sensed God wanted me to let them know that in spite of all the horrible hurt, He had not forgotten them. And even in their darkest hour He was hard at work on their behalf in ways they could not yet see but soon would.

I knew there would be days when Craig and Susan would feel lonely and overwhelmed by the loss of their beautiful eight-year-old boy, especially after the funeral when everyone went home, got back to their lives, and left them alone with their grief. I wanted to give them something to hold on to, a hope of a brighter day, a song to remind them of God's faithfulness.

Although "God Will Make a Way" was written for a desperate situation, I have never thought it to be a song of *desperation* but one of *declaration*. The lyrics do not present a question, "*Can* God make a way?" but rather a statement, "God *will* make a way." If He is God, then He has a way, in fact, *the way.*

## Yesterday, Today, and Forever

Have you experienced the sudden or tragic death of a loved one?

Are you going through a divorce? Or starting down the painful road toward one?

Have you or someone you loved received bad news from a doctor?

Have you lost a job or been thrown out of your career?

Are you entertaining suicidal thoughts you thought you'd never have?

Are you experiencing feelings of betrayal? Loneliness? Bitterness? Anxiety? Depression?

Are you worried and stressed out?

Maybe you have suffered at the hands of someone else through an injustice? Or by your own hand through addiction or self-sabotage of some kind?

If your answer to any or many of these questions is yes, even though you may *feel* that God has forsaken you and forgotten you, I want to remind you, or tell you for the very first time, that He has not. He has not, friend. Here is your new truth, your reality, and some good news:

> "And the LORD, He is the One who goes before you. He will be with you, He will not leave you nor forsake you; do not fear nor be dismayed." (Deuteronomy 31:8)

This is not a promise by some random deity but by the One who says He formed the world and your being as your Creator, who fashioned you in your mother's womb as Psalm 139 clearly states.

Isaiah 49:16 tells us that God has inscribed you on the palms of His hands. That is exactly why I believe that even at this moment, He is working in ways you cannot see to bring you hope and healing. I know He did for my family members, the Phelps. He has for our family of seven many, many times.

He knows where you've been because He is the God of the past.

He knows right where you are today and what you are feeling because He is the God of the present.

He knows what tomorrow holds because He is the God of the future.

For all these reasons, you can trust Him, whether you never have before, you did once upon a time but then quit, or you just need a fresh reminder.

## Uncharted Territory

Years ago I was sitting in the pastor's study of a little church just outside of Dallas, Texas. I had been invited there to sing on a Sunday morning and was having a few quiet moments alone waiting for the service to start. My eyes were drawn to a picture the minister had on his wall. The painting was of an old wooden sailing ship being tossed about on a stormy sea. The inscription at the bottom read:

> Those who go down to the sea in ships,
> Who do business on great waters,
> They see the works of the LORD,
> And His wonders in the deep.
>
> (PSALM 107:23–24)

I was immediately taken with and intrigued by the painting connected to the words of this powerful passage. Although I had read this psalm over the years on countless occasions, it was as if I was seeing the Scripture for the first time. The artist's rendering coupled with the psalmist's words created art for my soul.

What did the writer mean to "go down to the sea in ships" and "do business on great waters"? The sentence sounded at first like an amazing adventure to me. I not only wanted to see "the works of the LORD and His wonders in the deep," but I wanted to experience them personally. Not just by hearing the stories of someone else's journey but by knowing firsthand what life would be like on the deck of that great vessel.

From that experience, Psalm 107:23–24 became one of my favorite passages in God's Word. But I didn't realize in the moment that for me to fully understand the deep meaning, I was also going to have to experience the verses that followed. To experience life on that ship, I also had to be placed on the stormy sea.

For He commands and raises the stormy wind,

Which lifts up the waves of the sea.

They mount up to the heavens,

They go down again to the depths;

Their soul melts because of trouble.

They reel to and fro, and stagger like a drunken man,

And are at their wits' end.

Then they cry out to the LORD in their trouble,

And He brings them out of their distresses.

He calms the storm,

So that its waves are still.

Then they are glad because they are quiet;

So He guides them to their desired haven.

Oh, that men would give thanks to the LORD for His goodness,

And for His wonderful works to the children of men!

(PSALM 107:25–31)

The social media summary reads like this: "To see the works of the Lord and His wonders in the deep, you are going to encounter major storms."

The artist who created the painting did not depict the ship sailing gently through the water on a tranquil sunlit day. No, the ship was sailing on dangerous waves backdropped against a brutal sky.

Isn't it fascinating that we pray daily for only the peaceful, blue-sky days in our lives while the stormy seasons are where growth and maturity await us?

Psalm 107 reminds us that in life there are three types of people:

- Those about to go into a storm
- Those in the middle of a storm
- Those who have just come out of a storm

Right now, each of us falls into one of these categories. Because of this universal truth, we must constantly remind ourselves that when we go through a crisis, it does not mean that God has abandoned us. Notice in verse 25, it wasn't the devil who caused this storm but the Lord. "For He [God] commands and raises the stormy wind."

So often when we go through trials we assume that (1) God is angry with us because we've made a wrong decision and are suffering consequences, or that (2) God has abandoned us and we are being attacked. We ask God, "What did I do wrong? Where did I miss You?"

Often He answers those questions with, "Nothing. You didn't."

A decision to follow Christ certainly doesn't come with a guarantee that everything will always go our way and we will have smooth sailing on a peaceful sea throughout our lives. While this might seem wonderful, it is wrong thinking and quite simply unrealistic. In fact, walking closely with Jesus in this culture creates more storms!

Christ said, "I have told you these things, so that in me you may have peace. In this world you will have trouble. But take heart! I have overcome the world" (John 16:33 NIV). We cannot miss that while Jesus did promise His peace, He firmly stated we would have trouble as well. In fact, without trouble how would we be able to know we are experiencing His peace? Promises like these in Scripture are not that we will live our lives storm-free, but rather what God will do *in* and *following* our troubling times.

God will always use what we've been through, as well as what we're going through, to cause all things to work out for our good. Author and pastor Max Lucado paraphrased Genesis 50:20: "In God's hands, intended evil becomes eventual good." In talking about the life of Joseph, Lucado said:

> Nothing in the Old Testament story glosses over the presence of evil. Bloodstains, tearstains are everywhere. Joseph's heart was rubbed raw against the rocks of disloyalty and miscarried justice. Yet time and time again God redeemed the pain. The torn robe became a royal one. The pit became a palace. The broken family grew old together. The very acts intended to destroy God's servant turned out to strengthen him. "You meant evil against me," Joseph told his brothers, using a Hebrew verb that means to weave. You wove evil, he was saying, but God rewove it together for good. God, the Master Weaver. He stretches the yarn, intertwines the colors. Nothing escapes His reach.[1]

Sometimes the Lord directs us right into the middle of a tempest. Think how often in the Gospels that Jesus, always following God's will perfectly, encountered all manner of conflicts and confrontations. Rarely did He instigate them; mostly they found Him! In John 7:1, we read that the Pharisees "were looking for a way to kill him" (NIV).

When Jesus got into a boat with His disciples and said, "Let us go over to the other side," He knew full well that they were going to encounter a storm. So He decided that was a great time to take a nap. As the sky grew dark and the waves crashed against the small boat, in a panic the disciples woke Jesus up. They asked Him, "Teacher, don't you care if we drown?" There's nothing quite like a little manipulation with a touch of guilt from your friends, right? Christ got up and said just three words,

"Peace, be still." Immediately, the skies opened up, the wind died down, and the water became calm. Case closed (Mark 4:35–39).

———

In the storm you are going through right now, have you found yourself demanding, "God, don't You care what I'm going through?" just as the disciples did? Or even if you won't allow yourself to acknowledge His existence, are you blaming your troubles on an unknown outside force somewhere out there? What if instead of panic or anger or pride, you humbly invited Jesus to speak to your storm and say, "Peace, be still"?

After all, the real question is not if He can *calm your storm* but if you will *invite Him into your boat.*

Even when God does intervene on our behalf, we can often become cynical and questioning because we wonder what took Him so long. But the majority of the time, the real hold-up was we simply would allow no room for Him to work until life became desperate. I've heard it said that "to stay in God's will, we must stay out of His way." There is so much we blame God for that is just our own stubbornness blocking the road to our deliverance.

> THE REAL QUESTION IS NOT IF HE CAN *CALM YOUR STORM* BUT IF YOU WILL *INVITE HIM INTO YOUR BOAT.*

Do you suppose the disciples had a better understanding of Christ and their own faith after that encounter on the water? Though frightening and difficult to go through, storms offer opportunities for transformation. They can change us and make us stronger. That's

God's purpose for them. As a loving Father, He's not out to just rock our boats. He has a grand plan for something transformative to happen when people are "at their wits' end" and "cry out to the LORD in their trouble" (Ps. 107:27–28). When we finally admit to God, "I've run out of answers, I don't know where to turn, I'm at the end of my rope, my resources are depleted, and everything I've tried has failed," He steps into our storm with His peace.

## You Have Been Honored

Following Jeremy's funeral, I had the privilege of sitting at the piano and sharing "God Will Make a Way" with Craig and Susan. This was a very private and providential moment for us all. Just as we had so desperately prayed, God brought us His peace in our storm as only He can give through His Comforter.

As would be expected, for many months Craig and Susan struggled with the pain of Jeremy's passing and asked the very human questions, "Why, God? Why us? Why him?" They were literally living through Psalm 107 in their suffering and grief, "staggering around like a drunken man." But God heard their cries. He gave grace as they questioned Him. With time He calmed the storm, and the waves in their sea began to be still. As they looked to the Lord for His strength and support, the Phelps could "see the works of the LORD and His wonders in the deep."

Through the years, Craig and Susan have had many opportunities to share their story with others, turning their heartbreak into help for other families, offering encouragement to those who have lost hope after going through the tragic death of a loved one. As they have shared with thousands of people all over the world how God made a way for them, they truly believe Jeremy has reached more people through his death than he ever might have through his life. What a very difficult yet powerful statement for loving parents to make. But their perspective is not of this world, but of the heavenly kingdom in which they and their son reside.

Inscribed on Jeremy's gravestone are the following words from Isaiah 43:4:

> Since you were precious in My sight,
> You have been honored,
> And I have loved you;
> Therefore I will give men for you,
> And people for your life.

How about you? Are you ready for peace, for some stillness in your storm? Are you ready to find real and lasting purpose and become part of a far greater plan?

Whatever your need, God will make a way. You can discover His hope in your story.

*chapter two*

# THROUGH OUR SURRENDER

My mom forced all four of us kids to take piano lessons for six years. And I hated every minute of it. I can still hear her saying, "Donny, you wear the clothes we provide for you, you sleep in the bed we provide for you, you eat the food we provide for you. You *will* play the piano!" That was that, as they say. But I determined during those days that if I ever got married and had a family of my own, I would never "abuse" my kids like my mom had us. Well, when I became a father, my mom's attitude was ironically ingrained in me and all five of our children took six years of piano lessons. But to make matters worse, they also heard the same speech my mother gave me, many times.

Music always came easy for me. I won an award at age fifteen to study at the University of Minnesota for six weeks during the summer and while there took my first music composition class. One early assignment was to write two eight-bar melodies, which took me about five minutes to do while the other students struggled. The professor wrote on my paper, "Young man, you have a real gift and you need to pursue this." Funny how God starts dropping His markers on our trails early in life.

# Music, Mississippi, and Minnesota

I was raised in a Christian home where there were very strict standards and guidelines. My mother took a very dim view of secular (pop) music and much to her dismay, I played trombone in the school jazz band. She would tell me, "Donny, when you play music with a beat, people dance. And when people dance, bad things happen!" I think her belief was that church music was God's and any other music was Satan's. (I never felt good about giving the Accuser so much credit for most of the arts when he can't create anything on his own.)

I finally gave in to family pressure and quit the band. Even back then, the Christian witness that such a decision communicated to the other students bothered me.

I also couldn't go to movies. I was told that if Jesus returned for His Second Coming while I was in a movie theater, He would not take me with Him to heaven. Evidently location was more important than salvation.

When I left home for the first time to attend college at eighteen years old, a popular movie I was interested in was coming to the local theater. For several days, I prayed about whether to go. A belief indoctrinated into you as a child can be a tough thing to release. Finally, I wasn't hearing a no so I decided to take my chances on Jesus' return happening that night and bought my ticket.

The film was a racy barn burner called . . . wait for it . . . *The Sound of Music*. I. Loved. That. Movie! I stayed and watched it three times back-to-back-to-back. The screen was huge, the colors vibrant, the songs amazing, and the writing and arrangements awesome. Something connected in my spirit that night.

Up to this point, my career plan had always been to be a navy pilot, but because of my eyesight and the fact that I wore glasses, I couldn't get into flight school. Fortunately, I had a backup plan to work for the forestry service as a ranger because I loved to hunt and fish. To make a living outdoors seemed like a natural path for me. Maybe it was a response to having to stay inside for all those piano lessons. But by the time I was a senior in high school, because of my ability as a violinist, I was awarded a full scholarship to the University of Southern Mississippi. (You can imagine the cultural change moving from northern Minnesota to southern Mississippi. Up to this point, I thought Minneapolis was the Deep South!) To be completely honest, at this point in my life free college tuition was my only motivation to pursue music.

In addition to playing in the school's orchestras and for their musical theater productions, I played professionally in almost every symphony, ballet, and opera performance within one hundred miles of the school and traveled almost every night to a concert or rehearsal. I went to classes in jeans all day and around 3:00 every afternoon I changed into my tuxedo and headed for a concert somewhere. Returning to the dorm around midnight, I would study until 3:00 a.m., then repeat the same schedule the next day.

The struggle created by the theology I was taught in my childhood was still very real. Surrounded by incredible musicians and hearing the power and grandeur of Beethoven's Fifth Symphony or the beautiful melodies in a Puccini opera, I was sensing and feeling the power of God, in some ways for the very first time. When I listened to the incredible force of rising and falling chords and harmonies that created deep emotions within my soul, I struggled with these feelings and constantly questioned whether I was "in sin."

Playing and hearing amazing music felt so wrong yet so right all at the same time. Eventually I just gave up. I threw any dream of music into the religious trash bin, pulled out of the university, and got a job back home in Minnesota as a lumberjack. Yes, you read that right, I said *lumberjack*.

I put away the trombone, piano, guitar, and violin to operate heavy equipment deep in the forests of my great home state. The low pressure and regular pay were a welcome blessing. The only music I heard there was the chest-resonating low notes in the crack of a falling giant spruce or the whistling highs produced by the whine from the diesel engine of the bulldozer I was operating or the wind rushing through the tree canopy high above me.

But working outdoors in the mind-numbing winter temperatures of twenty to thirty degrees *below zero* made me rethink my life's calling. I distinctly remember the time I opened my sack lunch and my peanut butter and jelly sandwich literally had to be broken off in frozen, rock-hard chunks. I started to miss music and I knew I had to do something about the passion God had placed in my heart. Sometimes you don't know how much something means to you until you remove it from your life completely.

One day I turned in the keys to the log hauler, got in my car, and started driving back to where I had gone to college in Mississippi. After many long hours of driving and just a few miles from the university, I pulled my car off on the side of Highway 49. I knew in my spirit that I wasn't supposed to return there, but I was very confused as to what to do. After a moment in prayer, I sensed a distinct leading to turn my car around and start driving north again but with no idea where I was headed.

Logging in Minnesota? No. *Check.*

School in Mississippi? No. *Check.*

What now, God?

# Direction and Destination

I had a friend who was attending Oral Roberts University, so I decided to drive through Tulsa to stop and visit him. On an impromptu campus tour, he introduced me to the chairman of the music department and I ended up auditioning on my violin. While this all felt very random in the moment, God was making a way. He was providing direction for my life.

I often think about that decision to turn my car around, headed to some mystery location I didn't yet know. I think about the time God told Abraham to go "to a land that I will show you" (Genesis 12:1). He left, traveling not with a map from man but only by faith in God. No destination, only direction. Hebrews 11:1 talks about faith being "the substance of things hoped for, the evidence of things not seen."

My decisions to leave where I was in Minnesota but also to not return to where I had been in Mississippi worked together to create a tipping point in my life. My entire future was waiting for me at ORU in Tulsa, Oklahoma. Like the first flick of a domino to start the whole line falling, God needed me to *position* myself for Him to be able to *place* me where I needed to be.

If in the first chapter you answered several of my questions with a yes by saying you were ready for hope, for change, for a new direction, then I now ask you the following questions:

- What action do you need to take to position yourself for God to have the opportunity to place you where He wants you?
- Where do you need to start driving in faith with no destination but only in His direction?
- Where is your "land that He will show you," as in Abraham's story?

If you think this all sounds a little crazy, well, how have your other options been working out for you? Working in the frozen forests of Minnesota and sitting on the side of the highway in Mississippi, all I knew was where I *didn't* need to be anymore.

Sometimes God lets us clearly see where we *don't need to be* so He can show us where *He wants us to be*. We just have to admit that we can't stay where we are any longer. We must agree with Him that life must change and decide to cooperate with His direction. Then let Him be concerned with our destination.

There are times when we take inventory of our lives and call certain seasons "mistakes." But if no overt or intentional sin was involved, and we just made a choice that created a detour or diversion for a time, often God uses those circumstances to grow us in ways we might not have grown otherwise.

My escape into the woods became a clear path for God to drive home His intention for my life. I was able to clear out the confusion and chaos that can swirl around in a young person's mind, which certainly were in mine, to begin to head in the right direction. Those times can be much-needed seasons of change, rather than opportunities for second guesses and regrets.

ORU offered me a music scholarship and I accepted. My spiritual background fit well there and I knew I could receive a great Christian education as well as be involved in music once again.

In May 1971, during my junior year, I met Laura Shrock. After we got to know each other better, we began dating. Laura was raised in an Amish family in a rural farming community in Pennsylvania. (Yes, the horse and buggy folks who have sworn off modern conveniences.) But her father was excommunicated from their community and church when he purchased a power saw. His shunning meant he couldn't eat at their table and he wasn't supposed to sleep in the same bed as his wife.

Her dad had also gotten a transistor radio, which, of course, he wasn't supposed to own. One evening he tuned in and heard Billy Graham preaching the gospel. When the message was over, Laura's father went out into the orchard, kneeled, and asked Christ to come into his life, just as Dr. Graham had explained he could do. He prayed, "If this is real, God, I want it."

The man smoked a pack and a half of cigarettes every day. After trusting Christ, he immediately stopped smoking. When giving his testimony he would often say, "The sky got bluer and the grass got greener." His life was radically transformed, which eventually led him to take the entire family out of the Amish community. While Laura and I had very different cultural backgrounds, our religious upbringing had many similarities.

## Outreach and Inroads

At ORU I was working on a music education degree as a violin major, focusing on stringed instruments. During the last part of my junior year, I spent time observing orchestra programs in area public schools. I would visit a school that had a group of kids learning violin, an orchestra of about a dozen string players rehearsing in a dusty furnace room, and my entire life would flash before my eyes. Was this what I had signed up for as a career? As has been the case for so long in America, the fine arts programs were underfunded and understaffed. I started questioning my future as a music educator.

In Tulsa I met two men, Terry Law and Larry Dalton, who led a traveling evangelistic music ministry called Living Sound. The non-profit organization recruited young Christian singers and musicians who would raise their support and then travel around the country doing school programs by day and church evangelism events at night where Terry would speak and present the gospel. The daily events at the schools were intended to draw students to the church in the evening to hear the message of Christ. While there was no pay, all living expenses were covered.

After much prayer and more soul-searching, I decided to join Living Sound playing guitar, violin, and trombone. I wrote letters to everyone I knew asking for support to work with this group. Because of the extensive touring commitment and also to cut expenses, I sold my car. The donations started coming in and I hit the road with Living Sound. We did about one thousand concerts a year. Yes, I said one thousand! You're probably thinking, *Don, there are only 365 days in a year.* Let me walk you through a typical day for the ministry.

In the morning we would arrive at a school, set up, change clothes, play the concert, change clothes, tear down, eat lunch, go to another school in the afternoon, set up, change clothes, play the concert, change clothes, and tear down. And then we would go to the sponsoring church for dinner, set up, have an evening Bible study and prayer time, then play the concert that night with Terry speaking.

When students came forward to make decisions for Christ, everyone in the group would minister and pray with them. This was back in the day when many outreach ministries did these types of events and the schools often worked closely with the local churches. As you can imagine, this made for extremely busy days. And because there was no money for hotels, we stayed in the homes of people who attended the local churches.

Those years of actively serving and ministering to people on a daily basis knocked a lot of rough edges off of me as a young man. Those days humbled me in ways that I am so grateful for today. We would go at that schedule and pace for eighteen months at a time, never returning to our home base in Tulsa. We traveled on a bus—not a nice tour bus with bunks and a kitchen, but more like a Greyhound with rows of seats. Living that closely with a mixed group of peers allows you to see the very best and the very worst of everyone. Nothing stayed hidden for long.

Today with all the amazing technology and digital tools available, young people can create incredible music in their bedrooms inside a total vacuum with zero human interaction. But our true character is shown and tested when we take our art into the world and interact with others almost every single waking moment. I toured with Living Sound from the age of twenty-one to thirty-one with twenty other people—ten great years that God used powerfully in my life.

———

Laura and I continued dating seriously. She came out on the road to visit me and ended up helping with the Laws' baby. She served as a nanny during the performances and services. After two weeks, Terry told her if she could raise support, they would love for her to become a permanent member of the team. We were about to leave on a long tour to Europe and Africa, so this was an answer to my prayer that Laura and I could be together. She agreed, raised her support, and traveled with us for the next year.

In Johannesburg, South Africa, I sold my bass guitar so I could buy a ring. And in April 1973, I proposed to her, two years after I joined the group and one year after Laura joined.

The next month when we returned home to the United States, we were scheduled to be in my home state of Minnesota for two days to play a concert in Minneapolis. Ready to be married, we invited our families to join us there. That night during the service, Terry invited anyone who wanted to stay to attend our wedding immediately following. We were performing at a theater rather than a church, and we ended up having about a thousand people at our ceremony, many of whom we didn't know.

I played "Love Is a Many-Splendored Thing" on my violin as Laura walked down the aisle. We had two nights off in Minneapolis, then we went on to Des Moines, Iowa, for another day of events. A honeymoon was just not possible for us. So two nights after we were married, we were back to staying with church members we did not know—newlyweds in the homes of total strangers.

When we arrived at the host home that first evening, the people asked us, "So we hear you recently got married. How long?" We answered, "Oh, two days," as we prepared to sleep on those nice folks' foldout couch in the middle of their living room.

When we returned home to Tulsa, the home base for Living Sound, we had no home or apartment, so we had to stay with people there as well. Eventually, we bought a used mobile home for seven thousand dollars. When I was thirty-one, we decided to try to buy a house. The one we found was forty-nine thousand dollars. The mortgage lender said, "Mr. Moen, according to your tax records, you have lived below the poverty level for the past ten years. How do you expect to pay for this house?" Of course, we were declined for the loan.

But Laura and I never felt poor because we were rich in the things of the Lord—relationships, community, and ministry. Every day we lived out Matthew 6:33: "Seek first the kingdom of God and

His righteousness, and all these things shall be added to you." We sought God and let Him be concerned with the *things*. We lived a New Testament life as we traveled the globe.

Because of all the places throughout the world I was privileged to travel, I made many amazing friendships. Today, if you took a dart and threw it at a map of the world, there is a strong likelihood that wherever it landed, I would know someone in that location.

During those ten years with Living Sound, I learned to write and arrange music and, most importantly, I learned the Word of God. We had daily Bible studies, memorized Scripture together, and participated in in-depth discipleship programs. Laura and I were part of a wonderful family during the first decade of our marriage—the community of God with a built-in support system, reminiscent of the early church in the book of Acts.

## Recalculating Your Route

But to be clear, there were challenges as well. Especially during my early years in learning to seek God's will, I had many questions, chaotic times, doubts, fears, and "God, where are You?" moments. To continue our ongoing analogy, the Christian life is indeed more like a ship tossed on the stormy sea than a yacht tied securely to the dock.

In this chapter, I wanted to walk you through some of the early turning points I experienced as I learned to navigate life. From the confusing days to the courageous moments, from fearful choices to faith-filled commitments, God making a way in the life of a sinner is rarely pretty, certainly not easy, and in some seasons, downright messy. We only have to look at the lives of Abraham, Noah, Moses,

Joseph, Peter, and Paul—and all others we call heroes of the faith—to see that the common denominator in their victories was not anything they did, but what God did.

Maybe you feel like you always have to settle for second best on pretty much everything. I get that. I know how that feels. You may have convinced yourself, or maybe someone has told you, that you are "damaged goods" because of a failed marriage, bad business venture, abusive relationship, unplanned pregnancy, lost job, or any number of other difficult events. I have certainly had my own days when I believed this lie. But I want you to know that while someone or something may have broken your heart or your spirit, you are not permanently damaged. You are not second best. You are worth the great price Jesus paid for you. Your life has meaning and value.

In chapter 1, we talked about Isaiah 43:18–19. Let's take a look at those verses from *The Message* Bible:

> "Forget about what's happened;
>> don't keep going over old history.
> Be alert, be present. I'm about to do something brand-new.
>> It's bursting out! Don't you see it?
> There it is!"

Don't focus on what was. Focus on what will be. Have faith to step toward God's brand-new thing. A friend of mine once told me something that I have shared many times over the years: if you have a pulse, you have a purpose!

When you use a mapping app on your phone or a GPS in your car to navigate to a destination, you know exactly what the voice sounds like that is giving you direction. You also know if you make a mistake or miss a turn, you will hear, "If possible, make a legal U-turn" or "Recalculating the route." When things go really badly, the voice tells you to "proceed to the route," as if to say, "First, get back on the road!"

**IF YOU HAVE A PULSE, YOU HAVE A PURPOSE!**

The Holy Spirit of God, who comes through a relationship with Christ, is like an internal GPS who guides you into God's will for your life. When you make a "wrong turn" in a decision, He prompts you to change your course. If you don't change, He begins to "recalculate your route." You may have to travel a few rough roads to get back to the interstate, but if you will humble yourself and ask for help, God will hear your prayer, forgive your sins, and eventually bring you to your desired destination, sometimes to a far better place. God can turn your "plan B" back to His "plan A" when you hand Him the steering wheel, just as I did driving north out of Mississippi.

While the following simple truths may sound quite elementary, the more desperate you are for God's help, the better and more real these truths will become.

- God has not given up on you. Don't give up on Him.
- God is not finished with you. Keep moving forward.
- God has much more for you to do in this life. Have hope.
- God is working right now in ways you cannot see to make a way where there seems to be no way!

If you have connected to the stories I have shared thus far and the questions I have raised, and you are ready to connect with the four statements above, I invite you to pray the prayer that Laura's dad prayed in the orchard, a prayer like the one I prayed and have led thousands through:

*Heavenly Father,*

*Thank You for loving me even when I was unlovable. Thank You for sending Jesus to die on a cross for me because You loved me so much. I am a sinner, and I need a Savior. I have made wrong choices and made a mess of things. Lord Jesus, I am sorry for my sins. Please forgive me. Fill me with Your love. Fill me with Your Spirit. I surrender my life to You today and choose to follow You from this day forward through the rest of my life. Thank You for hearing me and answering my prayer.*

*In Jesus' name, amen.*

*chapter three*

# THROUGH HIS CALLING

Living as a married couple on the road with Living Sound for ten years, Laura and I experienced countless blessings, but there were two glaring negatives. The first was simply that we never had any time *alone*. During the days and evenings, we were always with at least twenty people. At night in strangers' homes, even though they were always absolutely wonderful people, we were rarely ever by ourselves. The second negative was that while we had purchased a mobile home in Tulsa, we never had time to live there. For the first time in our marriage, we were both beginning to feel the need to put down roots.

On one of our short stints off the road in Tulsa, I produced a record for a female artist. Her brother owned a major car dealership and liked my work. In 1980, he hired me to write a jingle for his company. He wanted the lyrics to mention all seven (yes, seven) brands of cars that he sold, from Jeeps to Jaguars. Always up for a musical challenge, I figured out how to fit every brand into the tune.

An ad agency heard my jingle and called to offer me a job. We felt this was the Lord providing an opportunity to keep me connected to music but allow us to come off the road. So I turned in my resignation to Living Sound, and we sold our mobile home, packed up what little we owned, and moved to Hollywood—not Tinseltown in California, but rather Florida, where I began to write advertising jingles for radio and TV. While I was still working in music, the methods and the motive were very different from those in an evangelism ministry.

# Jingles and Geriatrics

Finally with an income above the poverty level, we were able to buy a house—a home without wheels that someone couldn't hook up and drive away with in the middle of the night. My boss helped us find a reputable mortgage lender since this was our first major purchase as a couple. Remember the forty-nine-thousand-dollar home loan attempt when we were practically laughed out of the office? We were now moving up in the world. This deal beat our first try by *two* grand. We were approved and paid fifty-one thousand dollars for that home. I remember being so stressed about the amount of money to which I was strapping myself that I threw up all night before our closing the next day.

As you might imagine, getting off the road, settling down, and moving into our new home was an enormous culture shock. From twenty people to just us; from staying with families to being in our own bed every night. Personal issues and quirks that we had never had the opportunity to discover in each other—good, bad, and ugly—we now had plenty of time to see, hear, and experience. Many of the newlywed issues that most couples encounter in their *first* year, we went through in our *tenth* year.

Because finances were still very tight, we had one car. When I drove to work, Laura was left at home alone. All day. Those were tough and scary times adjusting to our first try at "normal life." Laura's sister lived in Okeechobee, so we would visit her when we could on the weekends. The gas to drive there round-trip cost thirteen dollars. There were plenty of times we couldn't go simply because we didn't have the money.

The house we bought was in a snowbirds retirement community. If you're under the age of forty, *snowbird* is a term of endearment for retirees who move south to Florida to escape the harsh, bitter weather in the winter and then go back home for the rest of the year. They "migrate south for the winter and then fly back home in late spring." Laura and I were now in our early thirties, living right in the middle of a bunch of retired folks. Our neighbors were in their seventies and eighties, all old enough to be our parents, if not our grandparents.

One couple became dear friends of ours and we spent many evenings with them playing cards and laughing about life. We will never forget our neighbors, John and Hyacinth Dearth, who were farmers from Ohio. (You have to be a character if your name is Hyacinth Dearth, right?) In the summer when they all left to go back to their homes up north, I would mow lawns for ten dollars each. Summers in that neighborhood felt a bit like a ghost town, strangely apocalyptic with us being some of the only residents left.

One New Year's Eve, Laura and I had gone to bed at about 10:30. Just before midnight, someone started banging on our front door. A gaggle of snowbirds had gathered outside, led by John and Hyacinth, demanding that we get up to celebrate. Sleepily, we got out of bed, got dressed, and joined the partiers.

—

My jingle job for the ad agency was set up so that I would record a demo—a rough version intended only for the agency to hear. Once they had approved and sold a package, the plan was that I would go into a professional studio and record a final version that would play on the air. But the salespeople thought my demo versions were good enough that they started selling them as final masters. Even though I protested the fact that they were literally selling my work short, they were clearly not going to stop. So out of my strong sense of musical integrity, I did what any true artist would do. I quit.

I immediately interviewed at another agency in Fort Lauderdale. The manager told me they had enough writers but they needed an assistant engineer in the recording studio. I felt like I had enough experience and could learn whatever else I needed to know, so I took the job. There were plenty of days I struggled because I was certainly in over my head. After finally convincing them that I was a much better writer than engineer, they agreed to give me a shot.

They put me up on the third floor of their office by myself with no piano. No instruments at all. For a writer, that isn't like tying just *one* hand behind your back, but *both* of them! Determined to be successful, when I got home at night I would write the jingle on my piano. During the day at the office, I would compose and write out all the band, orchestral, and vocal parts, string lines, brass lines, and so on with nothing to reference but my memory. On the upside, this equipment handicap greatly increased and enhanced my writing and arranging skills. God *never* wastes a thing.

The first opportunity I was given was the choice between four different jingle packages for four different businesses. Looking the information over, I decided to tackle them all. I finished writing them and went into the studio to record. After I turned in those completed packages to my boss, I never engineered again. I became a staff writer.

We would sell a generic campaign to a corporation, such as a banking chain, and then when we cut the vocals I would plug in the name of the city for each location. There was just one problem with that plan. The salesmen made all the money. I got paid per song. If I wrote a jingle and then we sold thirty versions with different city names, I got paid once while the salesperson got paid thirty times. Although we were no longer living on donations in Oklahoma, I was still a struggling—okay, yes, as cliché as it sounds, starving artist—in Florida.

# Recognizing a Revelation

My boss at the ad agency was Leon Golnick, a Jewish man. We were always keenly aware and very respectful of each other's spiritual beliefs. Over time, as we became very close friends, he became a father figure to me.

I had been working there for about a year when one day I was taking a break in the studio, drinking a cup of coffee and reading the newspaper. You know, just minding my own business.

Then God showed up.

One bold headline suddenly grabbed my full attention and pierced my heart. It read: "Rabbi Predicts Soon Return of Messiah." There was just something about those words that intrigued me, coupled with the knowledge of Mr. Golnick's beliefs, that God used to create a crossroads, a convergence of my music and my faith that was obvious and undeniable.

The headline shocked me. Right then and there in that moment

I knew I had to find a way to use my musical talents for ministry as much as possible. God was drawing me, inviting me, calling me to use my musical talents to bring people into His kingdom.

At the ad agency I was using my gift of music to make money and praying somehow God would use me. I now sensed that I had to surrender my music completely to God and let Him take care of the money. I knew my life focus had to change, which meant my career had to change as well. I had to return to Matthew 6:33: "But seek first the kingdom of God and His righteousness, and all these things shall be added to you."

In Christianity, we often make flippant remarks about knowing God's will—sometimes to be funny, sometimes because we are frustrated—by saying things like, "Why can't He just spell it out clearly for me, you know, like a newspaper headline or a billboard? Then I would know exactly what to do!" This story is proof that there are certainly times in our lives when He will do just that. I have no doubt that He did for me that day. God had a much higher purpose for those big, bold, black letters than an intriguing story lead-in for a newspaper. But then there are many, many more times, as is also the case throughout my life, that the word He brings is much more subtle, because He wants us to be tuned in to hear His voice. He wants us to be paying attention to His Spirit.

Have you ever had your own version of my headline moment in which God literally wrote His message out for you? Can you relate to God speaking to you through a very extraordinary and unexpected source, when and where you least expected Him to show up?

As Christ followers, we must learn to recognize His revelations to us. While we are waiting for answers, we must not stand still out of *fear* when He is calling us to simply follow Him in *faith*.

## Take Me Back to Tulsa

God once again showed Laura and me that His timing is always perfect. I called our friend and mentor Terry Law with Living Sound and told him about the headline incident and what the Lord had revealed to me. Terry said the ministry was at the point where they needed a new position—a composer, arranger, and supervisor to place musicians into their ministry that had now grown to four traveling teams. And he had the funds. Terry felt I was a perfect fit and the time was right. My title would be "music director." (In the music business, it's called an MD.)

> **WHILE WE ARE WAITING FOR ANSWERS, WE MUST NOT STAND STILL OUT OF *FEAR* WHEN HE IS CALLING US TO SIMPLY FOLLOW HIM IN *FAITH*.**

In the spring of 1981, we moved back to Tulsa. While we loved the snowbirds in Florida, we also had felt very isolated, especially in the spring and summer. This move would put us back into a strong spiritual community with old friends and solid fellowship once again.

While I didn't have to live on the road as before, I still had to travel all over the world quite a bit to visit the teams on-site and take care of any needs that arose. I recruited new singers and musicians to replace those who left. I handled all personnel issues of those on the road and had the authority to "hire and fire." I rehearsed people to get them ready to join the teams.

There were many times Terry and I had to leave to go to another country with little or no notice. One time he walked into my office and said we needed to leave for Russia *that day*. I went home, packed a bag, and left a note on the kitchen table for Laura that said, "Gone to Russia. Back in 10 days."

We quite often sent teams to the Soviet Union and I got to know many wonderful people over there. I even began smuggling in musical and recording gear for the underground church. Through an odd turn of events and the crazy connections God has always given me, I was asked to produce and record the English version of the 1980 Russian Olympics theme. Another team member from Living Sound translated the lyrics and I worked those into the rhyme and flow of the existing melody. Ironically, that was the same year the United States boycotted the Games.

When I started back with Living Sound, I had made the intentional decision to stop writing original compositions. After all, my job description was to find popular Christian hymns and songs and arrange those for the teams to perform. But through the time I spent writing jingles in a streamlined, almost assembly-line-style process, I had discovered a formula or a template for how to write a musical hook—a near-perfect marriage of lyric and melody that gets stuck in your head so that you'll be singing it the rest of the day. In fact, I had gotten good at hooks. And that scared me. In this new season of focusing on music solely for God's glory, I knew I didn't want to write *anything* outside of the power and presence of God. I also wasn't leading worship or performing music anywhere during that season.

## Messianic Manifesto

During my songwriting abstinence, I began to sense clarity from God's Spirit. I had a holy moment when I made a vow to the Lord that I never wanted to write a song unless the inspiration came from at least one of these four spiritual elements:

- Power
- Praise
- Healing
- Deliverance

While there's certainly nothing wrong with great love songs, they rarely change lives. While an up-tempo dance number may be perfect for celebrating at a wedding, no one senses the need for a Savior when the song is over.

There seems to be a pattern that the Lord often uses in our lives. He will birth a vision in us. Then there will be a point where we feel led to lay it down, even to the point of letting it die. Once we believe the vision is dead and gone, He will revive and restore it in us, often making our passion stronger than ever.

Abraham had Isaac, his promise from God, but then obeyed the Lord for the requested sacrifice. He died to himself and his dream by being willing to sacrifice the gift God had given him. Upon seeing him raise the knife above his son, God stopped him and showed Abraham the ram in the bushes, the animal that would be the actual final sacrifice. There's the pattern—birth of a vision, death of a vision, rebirth of a vision. For Christ, it was His life, then the cross, then the resurrection. God uses this sequence frequently to refine and purify us into the certainty that what we are putting our hands to is truly His and not ours.

Clarity and courage come when we reach the other side of rebirth. My manifesto—power, praise, healing, and deliverance—came from my raising the knife on my own music. I don't believe that revelation would have come had I been busy writing hooks—Christian or not. God was in the process of rebirthing His vision to give His songs to me. And what I could not yet know—He was about to speak again just as strongly as He had in the headline to take me to an even deeper place with Him.

When I had talked to my boss and friend Mr. Golnick about quitting the ad agency to move to Tulsa, he asked if I would be interested in keeping his company on as a side job. With Terry's blessing, we all agreed on this arrangement, and the extra money would certainly help. Every couple of months, I would fly down to Florida for a few days and work on jingle projects for the agency.

On one of those trips following my fresh commitment to rely fully on God's Spirit for any music I created, Mr. Golnick came into the studio with a bank president to listen to a jingle package I was recording for him. During a break, the president shared this story: "When you first sent me the demo for this jingle, I played it over and over several times. I heard something special. I then took it in to my bank vice presidents and played it for them. We all agreed there was just *something different* about this music compared to anything else we had heard in the past. We all heard it and agreed together. We knew we had to buy this music."

After we left the studio, Mr. Golnick called me into his office. With a look of intrigue and bewilderment on his face, he asked, "What do you suppose that banker heard in your music?" Without hesitation, I answered, "He heard the Spirit of God." My friend looked at me and said, "You know, I think you're right."

That *something different* the bankers heard was a *Someone*; Someone who knows how to produce power, healing, and deliverance, even in something as unlikely as an advertising jingle.

To be abundantly clear, that jingle I had produced for the ad campaign was not a worship song nor did it have any spiritual lyrics. Yet as I have heard so many preachers and pastors say over the years, "But God . . ." I had just written a jingle for a bank, *but God* . . . When He steps into circumstances in our lives, He can do whatever He wants and speak to people in any way He chooses. That's what God certainly did to all of us in that unlikely circle of a Gentile musician, a Jewish adman, and a bevy of bankers.

But the bankers' response sent a divine revelation straight to my heart. God had spoken yet again regarding the direction of my music. I realized in that moment that I wanted to use my talents as much as possible to reach people with the gospel. The Lord was indeed honing His call on my life.

> **WHEN GOD STEPS INTO CIRCUMSTANCES IN OUR LIVES, HE CAN DO WHATEVER HE WANTS AND SPEAK TO PEOPLE IN ANY WAY HE CHOOSES.**

I certainly believe God can use His followers in any legal and aboveboard profession—as plumbers, bankers, clerks, lawyers, waitresses, or whatever a believer does. He uses artists and musicians who are His followers in secular or mainstream music all the time to be light in darkness. Some of my dear friends in the industry do exactly that. How else could you explain what God had done for those bankers and my Jewish friend? I didn't write a "Christian" song. But He infiltrated my work because I had committed it to Him.

God anointed the work of my hands because of the intent of my heart.

**GOD ANOINTED THE WORK OF MY HANDS BECAUSE OF THE INTENT OF MY HEART.**

What I created with His guidance wasn't about the inclination of the lyrics but about the invitation from the Lord. His Spirit on our obedience is always a difference-maker. His anointing on our efforts is always a life-changer.

## The Gentle Whisper

After the prophet Elijah had destroyed the prophets of Baal, he got word that Jezebel wanted to kill him. Ironically, right after seeing God do an amazing miracle on his behalf, the prophet became afraid and ran for his life. After forty days and forty nights alone, he traveled to Mount Horeb and went into a cave.

The Scripture states that God asked, resembling His question to Adam, "What are you doing here, Elijah?" As if God didn't already know, the prophet explained his life-threatening dilemma. What happened next is crucial for us to understand about hearing the voice of God and His calling on our lives:

> The LORD said, "Go out and stand on the mountain in the presence of the LORD, for the LORD is about to pass by."
>
> Then a great and powerful wind tore the mountains apart and shattered the rocks before the LORD, but the LORD was not in the wind. After the wind there was an earthquake, but the LORD was not in the earthquake. After the earthquake came a fire, but the LORD was not in the fire. And after the fire came a gentle whisper. When Elijah heard it, he pulled his cloak over his

face and went out and stood at the mouth of the cave. (1 Kings 19:11–13 NIV)

Often when we are afraid and insecure, shrinking back from why God has placed us on His planet, we want Him to speak in an earth-shaking, big-noise fashion as our screens blow up moment by moment with newsfeeds, emails, text messages, and social media posts. But the Lord comes to us face-to-face in a gentle whisper. My friend Dudley Hall told me something I will never forget: "If you want to hear God's voice, make a friend of silence."

Through the "rabbi" headline in the newspaper, God whispered. Through a banking jingle, God whispered. Through a Jewish friend's question, God whispered. The same voice that whispered that day outside the cave to Elijah.

For those of you who have not had this experience yet, or possibly it has been a very long time since you believe you have heard a clear word from God, I want you to look very closely at what happened in my story and in Elijah's. I want you to see how God created something that could not be explained away as some coincidence or fluke. There is no reasonable explanation as to why someone would sense *something* in a jingle to the point of wanting to know what it was. There is no reasonable explanation for three natural elements to occur in sequence, and then for a whisper to cut through the quiet after the storm.

The other side of my story is I had to be in the right place in my heart, soul, and mind to be able to see and hear what God was doing and begin to connect the dots of what He was saying to me. I could so easily have missed His voice for so many reasons. But the hope of Christ alive in my soul allowed me to live expectantly to then recognize Him speaking, whispering, through the circumstances.

With all I have within me, I want you to know right now that God desires to orchestrate these same sorts of miracles and visitations in *your* life. But you must live expectantly. Live in the hope of Christ. Live believing that through His voice, His Word, the Christian community, and circumstances that only He can create, God will communicate with you. And you can and will hear His whisper amid all the noise of this world.

# 3:00 a.m. Wake-up Call

I was about a year and a half into my work with Living Sound and still had not written any original songs aside from jingles. One night while sound asleep, I was awakened at 3:00 a.m. I felt like someone had literally shaken me. My eyes were wide open and my mind was quickly alert. While I have never heard the *audible* voice of God, there are a handful of times throughout my life when I felt like I may as well have, because the communication was so strong and so undeniable. That night in that moment, I clearly heard in my spirit, "Turn to Psalm 40, verse 3." The message was that distinct. I got up, grabbed my Bible, and did just that. I read:

> He has put a new song in my mouth—
> Praise to our God;
> Many will see it and fear,
> And will trust in the LORD.

Sitting there holding the Scriptures, staring at those four simple lines, I thought to myself, *What is this? What just happened? God, what are You saying? What are You wanting to tell me?*

The next morning I told Laura about my strange encounter with God's voice. I said, "Something happened to me last night. It was like an ordination and I'm not really sure what it all means." After Laura and I hashed out what had occurred, I spent time praying for clarity.

I knew my calling to abstain from writing for a season meant that if and when He did call me back to my songwriting craft that I needed to fully rely upon His Spirit, not my own ability. If there was going to be "a new song in my mouth" and "praise to our God," it could not be about an *acquired skill* but rather an *anointed service* to and from the One I "fear and will trust." The rebirth would be all God and stay all about Him from that point forward.

The headline, the banker's jingle, and now the Psalm 40:3 moment were a series of events in which God spoke—preparing me, sifting me, pruning me, and setting me apart for His work. He was working *on* me so He could one day work *in* and *through* me to a greater level. This intentional direction is the road I have traveled and what I have done ever since the culmination of these three ordained events. My life has been committed to one single and solitary purpose: the worship of the Great I Am to usher in His power, praise, healing, and deliverance.

While I have led people in singing to the Lord for decades now, all those years ago I came to realize that, as Christ followers, our entire lives are worship in so many different ways. When Laura and I are playing with our grandchildren, to God that is worship. When we get to drill another water well

> **AS CHRIST FOLLOWERS, OUR ENTIRE LIVES ARE WORSHIP IN SO MANY DIFFERENT WAYS.**

in Africa, we are worshiping. When I sit with a friend over coffee and tell what God is doing in my life, I am worshiping. When our lives are operating in His Spirit and we are living in His truth, we are worshipers all day, every day and night.

# His Heart, Your Hands

God has placed my hands on the piano keys, and He has most certainly placed something that is personal, unique, and special in your hands as well, through which you can worship Him and bring glory to His name. This is also a pattern of how He works in and through us.

Noah had a hammer.
Abraham had a ram.
Moses had a staff.
Rahab had a scarlet cord.
Joshua had a shout.
Gideon had a trumpet.
David had a slingshot.
Mary had a baby.
A little boy had a lunch.
A widow had two coins.
A woman had a jar of perfume.
Jesus had a cross.

When God molds each one of us in our mother's womb, He plans to place something in our hands that we will use for Him.

Maybe today you know exactly what He has provided and you have been faithfully wielding your gift for God's glory in your circles of influence for many years. Bravo! May the days ahead increase your boundaries and expand your territory to bless God and all those around you as you serve in His name. May you stay inspired and be spurred on to even greater works.

Perhaps you discovered God's gift that He placed in your hands many years ago, but something,

> **WHEN GOD MOLDS EACH ONE OF US IN OUR MOTHER'S WOMB, HE PLANS TO PLACE SOMETHING IN OUR HANDS THAT WE WILL USE FOR HIM.**

someone, or some unfortunate circumstance, regardless of fault, stole it from you, cheated you, or simply distracted you. No matter the reason your hands are now empty, this can be the moment you choose to take it back up, to reach out and receive once again what God has always intended for you to hold for His glory. Let no enemy, no lie, no false accusation against you as a child of God hinder you from receiving your inheritance that He chose for you from the foundation of the world.

Finally, you may already be a Christian or have just become one, or maybe you have just prayed the salvation prayer for the first time in the previous chapter, and have yet to discover what God has in store for you. Your hands may be empty now, but you are ready for God's will to be revealed as to His calling in your life. Follow Him and He will show you His plans, just as you see what happened in my life. Immerse yourself in His Word that is filled with promises for you.

I will always remember the day I was headed out the door with my briefcase in hand to go on a sales call. I stopped in our hallway as

God spoke to my heart. Right then and there, I made the decision to follow God's call on my life to be a songwriter. I vowed to the Lord not to do anything else solely for the purpose of making money. Setting the briefcase down, I went straight to my piano and began to write. I knew in that moment everything I would do moving forward would have to be about my calling from Him. In the next couple of hours, I wrote the song, "Here in Your Presence."

> *Here in Your presence, beholding Your glory*
> *Bowing in reverence, we worship You only*
> *Standing before You*
> *We love and adore You*
> *Oh Lord, there is none like You*

To write those words that thousands of believers around the world would sing out in worship, I had to trade what I had in my hand for what God had willed for me from His own hand.

Here is a prayer for you regarding your own calling:

*Lord,*

*I surrender to Your will. I submit to Your plans. I can't do this by myself. So according to Your Word, I am calling to You right now and seeking You with all my heart. Give me Your hope. Lead me to my future. Tell me those great and mighty things I don't know. I want to listen to what You have to say. Please hear my prayer and show me Your way.*

*In Jesus' name, amen.*

*chapter four*

# THROUGH OUR TRIALS

Laura and I were married in 1973. During our third year of marriage, while on the road with Living Sound around 1976, we decided we were ready for a child. Keeping this decision to ourselves, we began to try to get pregnant.

When a young couple decides to start a family, typically there is a subtle but expectant assumption that a pregnancy will occur rather quickly. In fact, there is often a lot of stress in the first few years for any couple when they work to *not* get pregnant before being ready. But for us, once we started "trying," a few weeks passed, and then a few months. *Okay, so it's taking us a little longer than some folks, but it's all in God's timing, right?*

Before long, a year had gone by and nothing. No pregnancy. Then another year passed. And another. The physical, emotional, and spiritual questions started to pile up.

Is one of us the issue, or both of us?

Will this stress and hurt start to affect our marriage?

Why is God not blessing us?

I had claimed Psalm 127:3 (GW) for Laura and me: "Children are an inheritance from the LORD. They are a reward from him" as well as Psalm 128:3 (GW): "Your wife will be like a fruitful vine inside your home. Your children will be like young olive trees around your table." But where was our "inheritance from the Lord"? Where were our children "like olive trees around our table"?

Why do some people get pregnant one night in the back of a car during a meaningless fling and here we were married, serving God, praying, and hoping every day with nothing but the best intentions?

And then the entire experience just begins to get awkward, like a not-so-subtle irritation that slowly begins to hurt. Bad. Like a rock in your shoe, the rest of your life is good but that one place just keeps reminding you something is wrong. Every couple you hear about who has a baby reminds you that you don't, and can't. Walking through a church nursery upsets you because it's so obvious God answers other people's prayers. Mother's Day celebrations always made us feel out of place, seeing all the young mothers and mothers-to-be who were recognized. We, of course, were happy for every new life God created, but any reminder of what was so glaringly absent in our lives was painful.

Our families asked us all the time, "So, when are you two going to have kids?" When we were on the road and meeting new people every day, staying in the homes of godly, Christian folks who loved the Lord, the conversations often went like this: "So how long have you two been married?" When we answered, the very next question would be something like, "Well, are you planning on starting a family soon?" or a comment like, "I'm sure you're ready to settle down and have some kids." We were, but couldn't say that to anyone because we didn't want to have an extended conversation about our situation, especially with strangers we were with for only a few hours. So we would somehow manage to just laugh it off.

We knew we couldn't blame anyone for our hurt. The people on the road had just met us and didn't realize we had heard the same questions and comments every day and every night in all the cities on the tour. But let me tell you, the questioning got old and was really tough to deal with in the midst of our struggle. Those constant conversations became our cross to bear. After a while, even our families gave up asking.

One of the unfair assumptions people often make is that a childless couple cannot possibly be happy in their marriage. While certainly there is a melancholic aspect in being ready for a child and not having one, nothing could have been further from the truth for Laura and me. We had a strong, growing love and we very much enjoyed traveling all over the world together doing ministry. We worked hard to present a genuinely united front so people wouldn't make that judgment about us, because it just wasn't true.

## There's Nothing We Can Do

There were a couple of times Laura missed her period and we wondered if she was pregnant. Then when she did finally start, we questioned whether she had miscarried a child. Back in that day, pregnancy tests were expensive and most people didn't go to the doctor in the early stages. We could never be completely certain whether she was pregnant and had miscarried, or if her period was just delayed for some unknown reason.

Feeling the initial excitement of expecting a child and then finding out nothing is there dashes all hope. It's easy to start telling yourselves not to get your expectations up. You become more and more guarded about feeling any emotion related to a pregnancy, only adding to the disappointment and questions you already have. *Why did this happen? Why did You allow this, God? Why us? Did we do something wrong?* Many couples suffer in silence from this unspoken heartache, just as we did. Sadly, some marriages don't recover. You don't realize how many people have dealt with this deep hurt until you finally open up and share with other couples. Then you find out how many have experienced miscarriages and childlessness but never talk about it.

At the encouragement of Laura's sister and her husband, who is a medical doctor, we finally went to see an infertility specialist. We kept this very private because we didn't want people saying, "Poor Don and Laura, they're so unhappy and so desperate to have kids." The doctor suggested that Laura begin taking a drug called Clomid that cost five dollars per pill. At that time for us, the total for this treatment was an enormous amount of money. Along with the medication came the task of taking Laura's temperature and trying to identify the five days each month when she ovulated. During that time I was touring, so we spent a lot of money flying Laura to be with me for those five days. The expense was hard on us, but we somehow managed to eventually come up with the money.

Finally, the doctor recommended that Laura have a laparoscopy, a minimally invasive surgery using a scope that allows for a detailed view of all the reproductive organs. She also had a D&C. Following those procedures, they told us they couldn't find any signs of ovulation. And then he said the words you *never* want to hear from any doctor for any reason: "There is nothing more we can do."

Exhausted with the process, Laura asked me one day, "Do I have to do this anymore? I'm just tired of it." I agreed with her, so she stopped taking the pills. We stopped going to the doctor and accepted the reality that we might never have children of our own.

Eight years went by. Two possible miscarriages. Lots of money spent on a specialist for tests, medications, and surgery. Still no child. Lots of questions. No answers.

After about another year and a half, I received a call out of the blue from a pastor friend in Boise, Idaho. He told me there was a young girl in their church who was pregnant and she wanted to have the baby—a little girl—but was going to put her up for adoption. As they were praying about what to do, the Lord brought our names to them. They were aware that we wanted children and asked if we would consider adopting this baby girl. Having never thought about this option before, we both felt in our spirits that we needed to pray about it. Of course, we wondered if this could be God's plan to give us children. We asked them to give us a week. Maybe this was His answer for us as it has been for so many Christian families.

I already had a trip scheduled for Living Sound that week for me to go to Bristol, England. While there, I called Laura to check on her. At the end of the conversation, I said, "I love you."

She answered, "We love you too."

In a split second, I thought to myself, *We? Why did she just say "we"?* So I asked, "Laura, what do you mean by 'we'?"

A bit puzzled herself, she said, "I don't know."

I pressed her: "Do you think you're pregnant?"

She answered, "I don't know."

I asked the only question I knew to ask next: "Have you had a period?"

She paused a moment, then answered, "No."

To be clear in communicating the dynamics of this international exchange, that question from me and answer from her had occurred plenty of other times through the years. Laura not having her cycle wasn't necessarily a confirmation to us. When I got home from England, we went to the store right away and bought a pregnancy test. The result was positive. Laura was pregnant! This meant that she was expecting when our friends called us about the adoption—people who had been praying for us for a very long time to be able to have our own child.

Wanting to be very careful about getting our hopes up only to have them dashed yet again, we played it safe and waited a while to get an official answer. A while meaning four months! Feeling we had waited ample time, Laura wanted to go to a pregnancy testing center where they could tell you in person if you were pregnant, rather than notifying you through the mail. So we went to the Tulsa County Health Department. I especially looked really out of place. I was wearing a coat and tie, and, well, let's just say no one else was dressed like that.

Laura went back to the examination room and after about thirty minutes she returned to the waiting area with the nurse. Both had big grins on their faces and the nurse said out loud, "Congratulations! You're going to be a daddy!" I was a bit embarrassed and looked around the waiting room to see expressions of shock on faces as if everyone in there was thinking, *And you're happy about this?!* Of course, I was ecstatic and had a huge grin on my face!

## Why Should We Keep Praying?

In October 1984, after eleven-and-a-half years of being married, trying to get pregnant for eight years, and seeing fertility specialists for three years, we had our first child, Melissa. I was thirty-four and Laura was thirty-two.

During those many years and through all those disappointments, we had most definitely given up hope of ever having a baby. We had resigned ourselves to the fate of being childless. The older we got, the harder it got. The longer our circumstances didn't change, the more awkward the questions became regarding starting a family. But here's the key I want you to focus on: we never stopped praying for God to give us children. Our faith was wavering, but we still prayed. I think I should repeat that simple but profound statement again for this spiritual truth to sink deep into your spirit: *though our faith wavered, we still prayed.*

In our fast-food, next-day-air, digital-delivery, I-need-it-right-now world, we associate giving up hope and lacking faith with the obvious conclusion of "Why should we keep praying?" It seems like a natural progression: Give up hope. Give up faith. Give up praying.

Following is an incredible exchange between Jesus and the father of a demon-possessed child:

> **THOUGH OUR FAITH WAVERED, WE STILL PRAYED.**

> So He asked his father, "How long has this been happening to him?"
>
> And he said, "From childhood. And often he has thrown him both into the fire and into the water to destroy him. But if You can do anything, have compassion on us and help us."
>
> Jesus said to him, "If you can believe, all things are possible to him who believes."
>
> Immediately the father of the child cried out and said with tears, "Lord, I believe; help my unbelief!" (Mark 9:21–24)

There is an important connection we must make here with those places in our lives where we have given up on ever getting an answer. The man said, "*If* You can do anything, have compassion and help us." Jesus responded by saying, "*All* things are possible with belief."

The father uttered one of the best prayers ever recorded in Scripture and one we should apply often in our seemingly hopeless circumstances: "Lord, I believe; help my unbelief!" The man was saying, in essence, "Please take whatever belief I do have and then, Jesus, You'll have to provide the rest!" Jesus responded by healing the man's son. This is such a great prayer for our lives, no matter the source of our hopelessness and faltering faith.

Laura and I had to come to the place of giving God whatever faith we had on any given day and then praying for His strength and grace to provide what we lacked. We had to come to the place where we could say, "Our God is a good God even if we never have children." We had to come to the place together that Job did when he declared: "Though He slay me, yet will I trust Him" (Job 13:15).

Plenty of wonderful, godly people pray for children who never come. Some of those folks do end up adopting, seeing God's heart and hand revealed in their lives through taking in someone else's child as their own. Other couples pursue ministry together that a family with children might have difficulty being able to do. But regardless of the outcome, our role as God's children is to keep on digging deeper and deeper into our relationship with Him, to believe, and then to pray for help in our unbelief.

## Prayer as a Spiritual Weapon

I want to ask you a deeply personal question. Maybe you have never experienced a miscarriage or the pain of being childless, but you have certainly gone through difficult trials and your own brand of personal pain. You may be right in the midst of something tragic right now. Whatever has hurt you, devastated you, knocked you down on the floor, have you come to the place where you have stopped believing and quit praying?

Think about this: What if when you stopped praying, your answer was 95 percent there? A week away? A day away? An hour away? But the enemy convinced you that God is not a good God and He would *never* answer your prayer. The enemy manipulated you to stop asking altogether, which most certainly created distance in your relationship with your heavenly Father. And then because of the severity of the battle in the spiritual realm for your life, the distance between you and your answer also began to widen. The enemy's scheme is always the same, and his only goal is to sever you from God.

—

Suddenly, a hand touched me, which made me tremble on my knees and on the palms of my hands. And he said to me, "O Daniel, man greatly beloved, understand the words that I speak to you, and stand upright, for I have now been sent to you." While he was speaking this word to me, I stood trembling.

Then he said to me, "Do not fear, Daniel, for from the first day that you set your heart to understand, and to humble yourself before your God, your words were heard; and I have come because of your words. But the prince of the kingdom of Persia withstood me twenty-one days; and behold, Michael, one of the chief princes, came to help me, for I had been left alone there with the kings of Persia." (Dan. 10:10–13)

This amazing passage teaches us a great deal about the connection between prayer and spiritual warfare. God heard Daniel's request and sent the answer right away, but a battle ensued in the heavenly realm between the angels and the forces of darkness to stop God's messenger from coming to him. Verse 13 tells us that the fight lasted for twenty-one days until the archangel Michael was dispatched to help. He was evidently outnumbered by the kings of Persia and needed reinforcements to prevail.

Just because you don't have your answer does not mean the answer has not been given or is not on its way. Let this passage encourage you to pray and keep praying. We must outlast the enemy of our souls and not quit before God brings the battle to an end. We must grasp the deep truth that prayer is one of our most powerful weapons. We must use prayer to fight in the spiritual realm that affects our physical, mental, and emotional life every day.

We will prevail in our trials in, by, and through the power of prayer.

## Babe on the Bathroom Floor

As for Laura and me, God did answer our prayers and blessed us with four more children. We did eventually see Psalm 127:3 and Psalm 128:3 come to pass in our home. In fact, within seven and a half years, between October 1984 and February 1992, we had five children.

Melissa was born October 4, 1984, in Tulsa.

Michael was born December 16, 1985, in Tulsa. We were so surprised to find out that we had a son! He would be the first Moen grandson to carry on the name from my dad and his father and mother who emigrated from Norway in 1905. I remember bringing him home from the hospital and feeling that I needed to do something special to commemorate the occasion. I decided to create a "Norman Rockwell" moment. I put on my flannel shirt, started a fire in the fireplace, took out my Bible, and read to Michael as I cradled him in my rocking chair.

We were so broke that we couldn't pay our hospital bill, but with God's help and fifty dollars per month, we finally made the last payment when he was four and a half years old. I remember the day well, celebrating with Laura and saying, "We finally own our son! He's paid off!"

Rachel was born November 11, 1988.

John was born March 17, 1990.

James (Donald James Moen II) was born February 20, 1992.

The last three were born in Mobile, Alabama, while I was working for Integrity Music.

—

At 7:00 a.m. on John's due date—March 17, 1990—Laura told me she was having contractions. I went downstairs and called a couple of our lady friends to come over to watch the kids while we went to the hospital. When I got off the phone, I went back upstairs to find Laura kneeling on the bathroom floor, obviously in pain. She was having a really hard contraction, and her water had broken. Melissa and Michael (five and four at the time) were there with me. I told them, "Quick, help me get a towel under Mommy." We helped Laura lie down on the bathroom carpet.

Since Laura seemed to be peaceful, the kids went back downstairs to watch a Saturday morning cartoon. (Mom having a baby on the bathroom floor upstairs or cartoons downstairs? Downstairs wins.)

Suddenly, I could see the baby's head crowning. But I was still thinking to myself, *This moment will pass, and we'll get in the car like normal people and drive to the hospital to have this baby.*

Without Laura ever saying a word or making a sound, suddenly I saw the baby's head coming out, and I shouted, "What should I do?!"

She calmly answered, "Catch it."

Like any good husband, I listened to my wife's instruction and did as I was told. But then I realized that the umbilical cord was wrapped around the baby's neck not once, but twice. His face was turning blue from the cord strangling him. I shouted to Laura, "The cord is wrapped around his neck!"

She stayed calm and said nothing, but in that instant, I suddenly knew what to do. Don't ask me how, but it was as if *Someone* was standing over my shoulder telling me exactly what to do.

I reached down and grabbed hold of the cord and methodically untangled it from the baby's neck once, then twice, and within seconds he slipped out and I was holding our baby boy in my hands!

As I was counting his fingers and toes, Melissa and Michael came back upstairs, as their cartoon had obviously ended. I asked Michael to give me the used hand towel hanging on the rack. I wrapped the baby up and laid him on Laura's chest with the cord still attached.

Just then, I heard our youngest, Rachel, crying from her crib. I quickly went to get her so she could join the Moen welcoming party in the master bathroom. With the three siblings now sitting around Laura and the baby, I said, "Look, kids! You have a new little brother!"

I grabbed our camera and took some pictures of Laura holding her newborn son with our three other children surrounding her. This had all taken place within about five minutes.

About that time, I heard a knock on the door. It was our friends coming by to watch the children while we went to the hospital. I went downstairs to open the door and said, "You missed everything! We have a new baby boy!"

I'm a bit of a practical joker, so of course they didn't believe me, and I took them to see for themselves. Finding that I was not kidding at all, one friend just said, "Praise the Lord!"

By this time I was starting to shake, and I asked, "Don't you think we should call 911?"

The friend answered, "Well, Laura looks fine and the baby looks good, so let's deliver the placenta."

She had had several children at home and was well qualified to help in this situation. She told me to get a string and scissors and boil them in hot water. I wasn't thinking very clearly at this point and had no idea where we might have any string. Michael spoke up and told me there was some in the toy box, tied onto a little school bus he had been pulling around the house. Gathering the contents, I threw everything into the water to boil. I helped our friend as we cut the cord and delivered the placenta.

A friend who was a doctor heard the news and stopped by the house to make sure everything was okay. He agreed there seemed to be no need for Laura to go to the hospital and all seemed to be well.

We named our son John Luke and took him to the hospital eight days later to be circumcised. By the way, I saved about eight thousand dollars by delivering him at home. No four years of fifty-dollar payments for this child.

Though he is now an adult, I still love telling John his birth story. What a miracle and what memories we made that day!

Back at kindergarten, our oldest daughter, Melissa, wrote a story about our family adventure for her teacher: "My mommy had a baby.

His name is John. He was born on the bathroom floor. It made a big mess. But my daddy cleaned it up."

One of the greatest things about this entire experience is that on Johnny's birth certificate, the information reads: "Attending Physician: Don Moen." When I have shared this story over the years with doctors I have met, they have all responded with something like, "Wow! What a high-risk situation for the mother and baby."

While we experienced five miracles of birth, the fourth one certainly added more drama to the story line.

## The Truth of Our Trials

After James was born, we were surprised to find out that Laura was pregnant again, but we lost them to a miscarriage. We believe that pregnancy was twins. We had already told the children Laura was pregnant but hadn't said anything to the rest of our family yet.

While we have five children on earth and now grandchildren, too, we know we have children in heaven as well. That's hard to wrap your heart around. I still have no explanation or answers for tough and trying circumstances like this for any of us. But we thank God every day for the blessing of life and our family. We also thank God for how He has used our story to impact so many others by offering hope, help, and healing to people all over the world to keep going, to keep believing, and to keep praying.

Many years before we had children, a prophet prayed for all of us in Living Sound after a concert in Scottsdale, Arizona. When it was Laura's turn, he said, "I see you giving birth to a child. In fact, I see you giving birth to many children. I see an international family. The children you have will not stop you from continuing your international travels; in fact, they will go with you."

Can you imagine what we both felt when we heard those words? Could we trust this word? Was God just teasing us?

That exchange had been recorded and we had a copy of the tape. Every once in a while, during those many years we tried to have children, we would pull out that cassette and listen to the prophecy with both of us wondering if this could really happen. We give all the glory to God when we say that *all* our children have traveled and continue to travel with us on ministry trips around the globe. What God has done is truly amazing.

In those early years, Laura's sister and brother-in-law, Susan and Craig Phelps, were two of only a handful of people we let into our private world, sharing the hopelessness we felt because of our inability to have a child. They prayed for us *every day* for more than five years! They are the ones who led us to the infertility specialist to try to get us the help we needed. But they are also the parents of Jeremy, who died tragically in the car accident. The people who sacrificially prayed for us and shared our pain for many years became our prayer focus as we shared in their pain when they lost a beloved child.

In 2012 I released a project called *Uncharted Territory*. On that album was a song called "Somebody's Praying for Me."

> *I've been spared by so many prayers*
> *How many times I could not say*
> *What a difference a prayer can make*
> *When it's offered up in faith*
> *God has always made a way*
> *When I didn't know what to do*

*Just when I needed a miracle*
*That's when your prayers broke through*
*Somebody's praying for me*
*Somebody's knocking on Heaven's door*
*Somebody's praying for me*
*Somebody's lifting me up to the Lord*
*Well, I knew it had to be*
*Somebody down on their knees*
*Somebody praying for me*
*Now I know that friend was you*
*You were the gift God gave me*
*'Cause when you prayed His love broke through*
*It was your prayer that saved me*
*Thank you for praying for me*
*Thank you for knocking on Heaven's door*
*Thank you for praying for me*
*Thank you for lifting me up to the Lord*
*Now I can clearly see*
*That you were the one on your knees*
*So thank you for praying for me*[3]

One of the ways God has used those many years of pain and prayer in my life and ministry has been to have me tell our story. Almost every night in every country where I lead worship at events, I briefly share our testimony to encourage people. I speak a word of hope over the hurting couples in the crowd, those whose hearts are aching in quiet devastation from a recent miscarriage, those who have given up on God granting a child and resigned themselves to a fate they believe has been forever sealed. I say, "If you're here and are still believing the

Lord to give you children, raise your hand. I have the faith to believe that God can do for you what He did for Laura and me." Then I pray a simple prayer.

Because I am often invited back year after year to some of the same churches and ministry events, I have had couples walk up to me with their babies who were born during the year(s) following my being there the last time. What a humbling privilege to hold someone's miracle in my arms and have them tell me how my words of hope and my prayer were used by the Lord to re-ignite their own faith and prayers and change their lives forever. When those wonderful moments occur, I thank God for using our painful circumstances of the past to challenge people to just keep knocking on the Father's door.

If you have resonated with this chapter because of your circumstances, I want to offer you that same prayer right now:

*Lord,*

*I ask You to give this couple the desire of their hearts. Heal whatever needs to be healed and fill their home with the laughter of their children. Thank You for a miracle. We give You all the praise and glory.*

*In Jesus' name, amen.*

I also invite you to claim this Scripture passage as we did:

Therefore it is of faith that it might be according to grace, so that the promise might be sure to all the seed, not only to those who are of the law, but also to those who are of the faith of Abraham, who is the father of us all (as it is written, "I have made you a father of many nations") in the presence of Him whom he believed—God, who gives life to the dead and calls those things which do not exist as though they did; who, contrary to hope, in hope believed, so that he became the father of many nations, according to what was spoken, "So shall your descendants be." And not being weak in faith, he did not consider his own body, already dead (since he was about a hundred years old), and the deadness of Sarah's womb. He did not waver at the promise of God through unbelief, but was strengthened in faith, giving glory to God, and being fully convinced that what He had promised He was also able to perform. (Rom. 4:16–21)

In the midst of our trials, the reality is that no matter how strong we may have started the journey, we can grow weary and eventually forget the truth—the truth that our God can create a world with a word, part seas, flood the earth, make shepherds into kings, make kings into fools, and turn derelicts into disciples.

> **OUR GOD CAN CREATE A WORLD WITH A WORD, PART SEAS, FLOOD THE EARTH, MAKE SHEPHERDS INTO KINGS, MAKE KINGS INTO FOOLS, AND TURN DERELICTS INTO DISCIPLES.**

What has become a reality in your life that you once believed would never occur?

What do you believe can *never* be a reality in your life?

I am telling you right now, standing with you and for you on the promises of almighty God, that your prayers are reaching heaven, going to the ear of a loving and gracious Father who desperately loves you. Keep praying for God to move. Don't quit. Don't stop. You may be a day away from your miracle. Your trials of today can become your truth tomorrow. Let the strength of God's Spirit pour this reality deep into your heart for you to rise up out of your troubles and believe the Lord of your trials.

**YOU MAY BE A DAY AWAY FROM YOUR MIRACLE. YOUR TRIALS OF TODAY CAN BECOME YOUR TRUTH TOMORROW.**

*chapter five*

# THROUGH THE
# MOVEMENT OF HIS SPIRIT

Years ago, Laura's sister, Susan, wrote a letter to us that shared a vision she had in which I was standing on a stage. The Lord gave her these specific words as well: "Don will be leading thousands of people into God's presence and writing songs that soothe the hearts of kings."

When Laura read me that part of the letter, I immediately responded, "Honey, your sister Susan is a great girl, but she's not a prophet. There is no way I'm going to stand on a stage in front of thousands and sing. I failed my speech class at ORU because I was too afraid to speak in front of fifteen students!"

But Laura finished reading her sister's letter: "Don's real strength is coming from you, Laura, standing in the wings of the stage, supporting him."

Okay, now *that* I could see!

God is faithful to bring about His promises and prophecies, even when we see no way they could happen. He has a journey prepared to get us there, and places people in our path to help us.

# A Righteous Relationship

In 1985, I was working in the office at Living Sound Monday through Friday every week and traveling with the founder and evangelist Terry Law each weekend for ministry. Terry is still one of my best friends. I would lead worship from the piano and he would bring the message. That year, just two days after Christmas, he and I were on a plane coming back to Tulsa from a weekend of ministry. I was becoming aware of how weary I was from working and traveling so much, along with missing the milestones of my young family. My son Michael was only eleven days old.

The proverbial candle that burns at both ends soon smothers out its own flames. I realized on that flight that something had to give. The grace that had given me the ability to travel every weekend had lifted and I knew I couldn't continue at the pace I was going. So I quietly prayed, "Lord, please take me out of this and let me be able to be home with my family."

Terry's wife had been tragically taken in a car accident three years earlier, leaving him with three young children. Because of his deep grief, he was about to give up on his faith and the ministry when Oral Roberts challenged him to get on his knees before God and continue to offer "a sacrifice of praise" in the midst of his questions, hurt, and pain until a breakthrough came. Terry responded, God spoke and healed his heart, and a ministry was relaunched with a new focus. His book *The Power of Praise and Worship* contains the cornerstone content of his life's message. Terry based much of his teaching on 2 Corinthians 10:3–5:

For though we walk in the flesh, we do not war according to the flesh. For the weapons of our warfare are not carnal but mighty in

God for pulling down strongholds, casting down arguments and every high thing that exalts itself against the knowledge of God, bringing every thought into captivity to the obedience of Christ.

Terry taught that the Word of God, the name of Jesus, and the blood of Jesus are three offensive weapons God has given us to defeat the enemy. These weapons are engaged through the preaching of God's Word, prayer, testimony, and praise and worship. The message resonated with people across the nation and around the world. Every weekend we were seeing dramatic moves of God as people grasped the vision that our worship creates an atmosphere for God to move in miraculous ways.

Terry was always a kingdom man who would not hold anyone back and wanted the best for everybody. He always preferred me to lead worship in any setting where he was ministering, but I always felt inadequate. I wasn't a great singer or a great pianist, and we were ministering at very large churches with outstanding musical talent, yet Terry constantly pushed me to excel as he challenged me in my gifts.

Once at Carpenter's Home Church in Lakeland, Florida, in front of several thousand people, I was playing "We Bring the Sacrifice of Praise" in the key of E flat. I knew I wanted the song to lift, which meant a key change to E, but as I went for it, I realized I couldn't play in that key. A moment of panic came over me and I broke out in a sweat. In a heartbeat, I decided I would just lift my hands and worship without playing and then transition again into the key of F that I could actually play!

Back at the hotel, I told Terry, "That's it! I'm not doing this anymore. I'm tired of being humiliated in front of thousands of people every weekend!"

Terry calmly responded, "Well, that's exactly what you need—a good, swift kick in the pants to get you doing what God has called you to do."

And that was the end of that conversation. Nothing more was said.

He believed in me when I didn't believe in myself. I would not be where I am today had Terry not pushed me to grow past my own limitations. He put a demand on my gifts. After being humiliated, or at least that was my perception, in front of thousands of people each week for about three years, I developed my own style. I'm not sure exactly how to describe what I do, but it was birthed from my being pushed outside of my comfort zone week after week for many years.

When Jesus first met Peter, he was just a loudmouth fisherman. But then there was that whole water-walking incident. When Jesus asked the disciples who He was, Peter was the only one to answer. There was that time Peter tried to tell Jesus he would make sure He wouldn't be killed and Jesus rebuked him. Peter was the one to ask the question about forgiveness and received the seventy-times-seven answer. Time and time again we see intense interactions between Jesus and Peter. But from Jesus' personal challenges and providential pushes, Peter was the one to preach and see five thousand people respond to the gospel. The loudmouth fisherman in Matthew became the articulate teacher in Acts.

A definite pattern that we see in Scripture and in the Christian life is that God uses key relationships to challenge us to go places we would never choose on our own. The right person whom God ordains and places in your life can accelerate your growth in every way—spiritually, emotionally, mentally, as well as in your gifts and skills.

Has God put someone in your life who is pushing you out of

your comfort zone? Challenging you? Be sure you embrace that person to receive all that God has for you. While the process can sometimes be difficult, the result will be worth every minute of energy and focus you give.

## GOD USES KEY RELATIONSHIPS TO CHALLENGE US TO GO PLACES WE WOULD NEVER CHOOSE ON OUR OWN.

Terry and I had begun recording a live worship service every quarter entitled "Expressions of Praise" to send as a gift to the ministry's donors. Seeing what God was doing in my worship leading and songwriting, and knowing he wouldn't be able to have the budget for where I would need to grow, Terry came to me and said, "Don, I will always have a place in my ministry for you, and if you want to stay here for forty years, you can. But you can't do all that God is calling you to do and what He wants for your life if you remain here."

After much prayer I knew he was right, and we agreed that June 30, 1986, would be my last day with Terry's organization.

We ministered in Minneapolis, Minnesota, in what would be our last service together. Afterward, we went to our favorite Indian restaurant for curry. Walking to our separate cars, I realized this was goodbye for us.

I stopped and said, "Hey, Terry, it's been a great fifteen years."

He looked at me, kind of surprised, and responded, "Oh, yeah, God bless you, Don. There will be a lot more to come, I'm sure."

And that was that. As hard as it was to walk away from my friend and his ministry after fifteen years, I knew God had answered my prayer on that plane ride six months before.

# The Birth of a Movement

Gulf Coast Covenant Church in Mobile, Alabama, was the head-quarters for *New Wine* magazine, with a monthly circulation of about eighty thousand subscribers, which focused on the teachings of five charismatic Christian leaders: Ern Baxter, Bob Mumford, Don Basham, Derek Prince, and Charles Simpson, the pastor at Covenant. These men were amazing Bible teachers with powerful messages that were published each month in the magazine. Mike Coleman was the editor and part of the executive team of the magazine, an outreach of an organization called Integrity Communications. They were all based out of the church in Mobile.

In 1984, Terry and I had been invited to their church where he preached his message on spiritual warfare and worship. The magazine decided to run a feature story for three consecutive issues on his teaching. The response to the articles was overwhelming, and people started asking to hear the songs of worship connected to warfare. To respond to the demand, Hosanna! Music was launched out of the magazine.

Terry and I were invited back to Mobile in July 1985 to minister at a conference for Gulf Coast Covenant Church. While we were there, Mike Coleman asked if I would be willing to lead worship on one of their bimonthly recordings that they would release in the Hosanna! Music Club. I agreed, but because my travel schedule was booked out so far in advance, it was almost a year before I could record with them.

In May 1986, before I left Terry's ministry the following month, I had recorded *Give Thanks* for Hosanna! Music. The project was released in January 1987. That opportunity was one of those moments that changes the course of your life forever. The company had started to take off, and I remember when they told me that *Give Thanks* could sell as many as fifty thousand copies. The title actually ended up selling more than a million copies, becoming one of Integrity Music's most popular releases.

A month after recording that project, I continued to write songs and began to help produce vocal and choir sessions for Tom Brooks. He began producing all their projects after he recorded a live worship event for his church, Grace World Outreach in St. Louis, Missouri, which featured Ron Tucker, Tom's pastor, as the worship leader. That project had been used to launch the new Hosanna! Music, through *New Wine* magazine.

I became a part of the creative team in picking the worship leaders to be recorded, planning the song lists, and scheduling the recordings for each release. The team consisted of Mike Coleman, Ed Lindquist (Mike and Ed were cofounders of Integrity Music), Gerrit Gustafson, Tom Brooks, and myself. We reached out to churches everywhere and asked them to send in cassettes of their worship music. As you can imagine, what we received was all over the map. Some were horrible quality but God's Spirit saturated the songs, while others were slickly produced but were clearly only a performance. We were seeking moves of the Spirit, not just church songs.

Hosanna! Music became *New Wine* magazine's fastest-growing subscription program. The concept mushroomed quickly as demand for new, fresh worship was very high in that season. Every eight weeks, we sent out a tape from various churches to the widely growing mailing list.

Every other month, the five of us would convene, most often at Tom's house in St. Louis, to plan the next project. We would begin each day with prayer, crying out to God for wisdom and guidance for the next project, asking Him to reveal to us what He wanted to do. There were many days that our prayer time lasted three to four hours.

I once heard a pastor say that the disciples prayed for days so that when Peter preached for ten minutes, God moved mightily in thousands of lives. Now, we want to pray for ten minutes and expect God to move for days and still reach thousands. We have it backward in our culture. I can tell you that our group prayed fervently and didn't stop until we all felt we had sought the Lord. I truly believe those prayer sessions were one of the primary reasons God moved through that ministry with the power and anointing that He did. We passionately asked and He answered in power.

We would eat lunch and then spend the rest of the time together listening to the stacks of cassette tapes that churches had sent in. We would rate the songs from 1 to 10, with anything lower than a 7 being thrown out. Anything *above* a 7, we would write the title on a whiteboard for final consideration. Throughout all those sessions, we listened to literally *thousands* of songs.

For every thousand songs we listened to, there would be about a hundred that we'd put on the "possible" list. Out of those one hundred songs, we'd use about ten. Of that ten, there would be one song that would rise to the top, connect, and impact millions of people around the world.

## Handling the Humbling

During the next year I began doing more work for Integrity as a songwriter, producer, and arranger, working closely with Tom Brooks, the senior producer. On one project, after sending a rough mix to the creative team for review, I got a call to stop work on the project immediately and come to Mobile as soon as possible to meet with everyone.

(A "rough mix" is where you get all the music levels reasonably set solely for the purpose of a handful of people hearing the project for reference.)

After they had expressed their concerns on the project, I knew I hadn't given them a proper idea of what the final songs could sound like and they were accustomed to hearing Tom's mixes that were closer to the final. They felt my work was subpar to the ministry's standards, so I was fired from that project.

Though I was very discouraged, Mike assured me that he was committed to me and wanted to make the relationship work. He saw something in me and felt God wanted me involved with Integrity. He said he felt God had told him to build a platform under my ministry. Like Terry Law before him, Mike was challenging and supporting me in the places I struggled to believe for myself.

For the project I was fired from, I had already scheduled a date for the choir to do the vocals on the recording in Tulsa. But I had to cancel the sessions and tell everyone that I'd been pulled from the project. That was one of my most humbling moments. I had no idea how this situation was going to grow and challenge me, which was God's plan all along.

Months later, I got a call from Tom Brooks, who was now producing the recording, asking if I would come to the session and conduct the choir. Though I was still dealing with the rejection of being taken off the project, I agreed to help him out. That day, as I drove up to the studio, my ego was struggling. I sat in my car and inventoried the situation. Now, instead of being the producer, I was "just the choir director," relegated to waving my arms before the entire group while keeping a big smile on my face to inspire everyone. I decided that I couldn't make this work. It was just too embarrassing. So I drove away.

I had only gone about a mile down the road when I began to feel very strange. And I knew that feeling all too well. The Holy Spirit was convicting me of my attitude. I knew that if I kept driving I would be making a decision that would affect me for the rest of my life. I pulled over into a parking lot and heard the Holy Spirit say, "Swallow your pride. Humble yourself. Go lead that choir in worship."

I turned my car around and started driving back to the studio. That moment was both a test and a turning point. And just as the Holy Spirit had warned me about what would happen if I had kept driving, the other side became true when I decided to repent—yes, I literally had to turn around—and be obedient. From that session, my relationship began to grow in a new way with Integrity.

I was asked to lead worship on another Hosanna! Music release and once again became part of the creative team. Eventually I was offered a full-time job as song development manager, which would mean uprooting my family from Tulsa and moving to Mobile. That was a huge decision for me and I needed some time to seek the Lord. While praying, I felt the Lord say to me, "You don't have to pray about this anymore. The decision has been made."

Misinterpreting the message, I called Mike at Integrity to tell him I would take the job. To my surprise, he told me that since they hadn't heard back, the job had been given to someone else. Disappointed and a bit confused, I responded, "Well, whenever there's an opportunity available there, I think it will be custom and tailor-made for me."

Mike responded, "Why don't you write down exactly what you would like to do here and let me see it?" He said he would do the same. We got together at our next creative team meeting to compare notes. Not only were our job descriptions nearly the same, but we had also written down the same title: creative director. The decision was made and in October 1988, I joined the staff at Integrity. Our family left Tulsa and moved to Mobile.

My primary focus was to find churches where a move of God was happening. It was interesting that when I would find out about a revival and movement in a church, I would also find fresh worship songs being born from the Spirit. I introduced these churches and their music to the entire team, and we would then attend their worship services and produce live recordings to release.

The day I was driving away from that studio was yet another critical juncture in my life when God intercepted me to put my heart back in line with His will. We have all heard the phrase "Don't burn your bridges." Had I allowed my ego to win in that *one moment* while driving away, I would have missed *thousands of opportunities* through many years to be a part of something special that God was doing.

No matter how we may feel about ourselves and our own gifts, we must never discount those who hear from God and speak into our lives, even when the words may be difficult to hear or the outcome may not be as we hoped, because we must always remember that God is at work.

King Solomon said it so well: "The end of a matter is better than its beginning, and patience is better than pride" (Eccl. 7:8 NIV).

*chapter six*

# THROUGH PROVIDING
# HIS PLATFORM

"Give Thanks" became one of my signature songs. I had discovered it in January 1987 at a Bible study in Texas. We had no idea who had written it, but people started associating the song with me. We just listed the credits as "author unknown." Three years later, we located the writer. But the traction around the world from that one song began to build a platform for me as a worship leader.

In those days, everything for Integrity was about the songs. We didn't focus on the promotion of artists, writers, or singers, but people were starting to associate us solely with worship. I always told people in those days, "This worship movement wasn't man's idea, but God's. Isaiah 61:11 says, 'God is causing righteousness and praise to spring forth to all the earth'" (author's paraphrase).

As pastors began to call and ask me to come and lead worship for special events at their churches, at that time I had no sense of calling to do that ministry. But one situation that got my attention was a request from an African American pastor from New York City who asked if I would be a part of their church dedication service. I wondered why he would contact me of all people to lead at his church, so I asked him, "Do you know who I am?"

He was perceptive and understood what I was really asking, so he responded, "I know exactly who you are. We don't want black gospel! We want worship!"

After hearing such an affirmative and direct answer, I responded, "Okay! Then I'll be there."

That Sunday at his church, I had some time before the service began. It was a beautiful day, so I decided to take a stroll down the street through the neighborhood. Before I could get very far, a couple of men ran after me, calling my name. When I stopped and turned around, they said, "Mr. Moen, we don't think it would be good for you to be walking around in this neighborhood by yourself. You'd better come back with us." The church was located in the Bedford-Stuyvesant area, known to the locals as "Bed-Sty," evidently a rough section of town. Realizing what they meant, I cooperated and walked back with them, thankful for their care and company.

**THE HOLY SPIRIT WAS USING PRAISE AND WORSHIP MUSIC TO BRING UNITY TO THE BODY OF CHRIST AND REACH THE WORLD.**

We had a great time that day glorifying God and giving thanks as we dedicated their church building. In moments such as that, I realize true worship transcends cultures, denominations, and generations. I've seen this firsthand on many, many occasions all over the world. Songs of worship were breaking down walls and becoming anthems for the church at large regardless of the dividing lines man had created. The Holy Spirit was using praise and worship music to bring unity to the body of Christ and reach the world.

People were constantly sending in letters to Integrity recommending churches and worship leaders that we should visit to hear the music. Every weekend I was flying somewhere to experience a worship service. Several people had contacted me about Ron Kenoly, the worship leader at Jubilee Christian Center in San Jose, California. Even while I was in England, someone told me about Ron. So I knew I had to go see this guy for myself.

When I visited Jubilee, Ron and I made an immediate connection and agreed to do a project together. His first album was titled *Jesus Is Alive*. The project was hugely successful on every level. We followed with a second project called *Lift Him Up*. On that release, we decided to take the traditional route and promote Ron as the artist, putting his picture on the cover. That was the first time Integrity varied from our proven model, which did not go over well with some folks. They thought we were moving from God-centered to man-focused, that we were not lifting up Jesus but Ron. That was not our intention at all. Ron's projects were so much in demand and so well received, we felt it was time to connect people directly to his ministry with Integrity as the label.

For *Lift Him Up*, we decided to release not only an album but also a live video of the event. The date was in November 1991 and the venue was the Chrysler Hall in Norfolk, Virginia. Because of recording and videoing the entire album, the budget was the highest of any project we had undertaken, so wanting to find a way to offset some of the expenses, Mike Coleman said, "Hey, Don, why don't you go out and warm up the audience for Ron? Since we have cameras here, we'll go ahead and record your set as well and release it as a separate product."

That is how *Worship with Don Moen* was created and produced—as a warm-up set for the *Lift Him Up* recording. For that first event, we only had time for a short rehearsal. The band and singers didn't know my songs well, but once we started worshiping, everything gelled and the music flowed beautifully. Among other songs that night, we recorded "Give Thanks," "I Want to Be Where You Are," "God Will Make a Way," and "I Am the God That Healeth Thee."

At the end of the evening, one of the marketing people asked me to sit at the piano so we could get a photo. Using his Instamatic camera, he snapped the picture that became the cover of that project. With no marketing budget and no album release plan, the video went around the world.

On that trip flying to Norfolk, the Lord reminded me of ten years earlier when He had given me His prophetic word from Psalm 40:3, "I have put a new song in your mouth, a song of praise to our God. Many will see it and fear and put their trust in the Lord" (author's paraphrase). Record companies have spent millions trying to market what God did for me on a shoestring budget. He keeps His Word. He *will* make a way. All I did I was just walk through the doors He opened.

## Comfort versus Conviction

Working at Integrity was my dream job. I loved being a part of all God was doing there. I had the privilege of connecting with incredible worship leaders, songwriters, and musicians from all over the world. By the fall of 2005 as I began to tour myself, I became aware that God was opening doors for me with my music. As I mentioned before, being an artist was not something I sought out. But I could no longer ignore the fact that God was giving me a platform beyond my role as a music executive, an opportunity to share His message of power, praise, healing, and deliverance through my own ministry. There was just one problem: *I wasn't paying attention.*

While I was well aware God was speaking, I was simply ignoring His words. But then over time I began to become *convicted.* When we initially become aware of a divine message, we often don't take responsibility for it. But when it starts to sink into our spirits and we feel conviction, we must decide to take action and make real changes.

When I returned home from one of my tours, I talked to Mike and told him what God was saying to me. I told him I had to make some changes, which likely meant changes in my role at Integrity. I talked about phasing out while still staying connected somehow as an artist. After much discussion, we agreed that I would stay on for two more years. I would continue to lead Integrity Music, focusing on signing the right artists and right songs to serve the church.

By that time, Integrity Media was a large umbrella company and the music division was only one of the parts. The idea was to take the worship label back to the beginning days when we were a launching pad for so many great songs from the church that ushered in the presence of God. That all went as Mike and I planned until once again, God intervened.

—

In March 2007, I was invited to Ghana, West Africa, to lead that nation's celebration event in giving thanks for fifty years of independence. I brought my full band and team, but as soon as we arrived at the venue, I sensed something spiritual that I had never experienced before.

Something bad. Something evil. I knew we were under some kind of spiritual attack and we had to pray and ask others to intercede for us. This was my first trip to West Africa, and I sensed a different kind of spiritual warfare. I told everyone on the team to contact every prayer group they knew to ask people to pray for us.

During our sound check, my guitar player reached down and touched a piece of equipment where there was an electrical ground loop. He was immediately hit with 220 volts and fell to the floor shaking, his hands unable to let go, locked up by the extreme voltage coming through his guitar. We had to literally kick his guitar out of his hands to break the connection. He just lay there, not moving. We were certain he was dead. I picked him up and began to pray earnestly for God to heal him. Slowly, he recovered, but he was badly shaken from the shock. The electrical problem was eventually fixed, but the concert start time had to be delayed by four hours.

After we returned home, I began to experience severe pain in both my feet. For almost a year, this made it difficult for me to walk. My drummer had a heart attack. My guitarist had a heart attack. My keyboardist had a heart attack. Three young men all had heart attacks within weeks of returning from Ghana. While all of them fully recovered, I knew beyond a shadow of a doubt these attacks were not coincidences.

The phrase "all hell broke loose" was definitely true of that trip, directly related to whatever spiritual force of darkness had come against us in Ghana. The Lord had my full attention, and I knew I had to make some changes. He reminded me of the parable of the talents in Luke 12, specifically: "To whom much is given, from him much will be required" (v. 48). If I was going to answer God's call to lead worship in the nations of the world, I needed to make prayer a priority and develop an army of prayer warriors to stand with me whenever and wherever I went.

Through the years, we have built a very large prayer team that is faithful to intercede for all God has us do. I have been out on tour with *no* prayer support and I have been on tour *with* prayer support and I can tell you, there is most assuredly a night and day difference—literal darkness and light. I determined to have people around the world praying for us as we led worship in the darkest of places. Once we were fully covered in prayer support, every trip was far more successful—spiritually and otherwise.

Through God's message to me, I began to see that it was time to leave Integrity Music. I needed to focus all my energy and time on my own ministry. By the end of 2007, I had left and launched out on my own. Staying at Integrity had the appearance of being the safest place for me. But when God calls us out and we don't respond, what was once secure can become stagnating.

Leaving something proven is a very difficult thing to do. But you cannot embrace a new thing while still holding on to the old thing. Stepping out of the boat into the stormy sea is frightening. Leaving your comfort zone will never be comfortable.

I recall in those days feeling very alone and afraid of the step of faith I had taken. Even though it was the middle of 100-degree heat in the Alabama summer, I remember continually singing the words from the Christmas carol "Away in a Manger": "Be near me, Lord Jesus, I ask You to stay. Close by me forever and love me I pray." Something about that simple song and prayer brought me great comfort.

**LEAVING YOUR COMFORT ZONE WILL NEVER BE COMFORTABLE.**

On October 14, 1947, Chuck Yeager was the first confirmed pilot to exceed the speed of sound in level flight, producing the first sonic boom ever heard on Earth. Prior to this achievement, he and other pilots had experienced unstable controls and terrific structural mishaps with the planes encountering severe buffeting and sudden nose-up and nose-down trim changes. But when Chuck was finally able to push through and break the barrier, he said his "X-1 no longer buffeted; supersonic flight was as smooth as could be." He was able to hold the speed for about twenty seconds, saying his "ride through the sonic wall was nothing more than a poke through Jell-O."[2]

When God calls us to push through and attempt new things for Him and by Him, most people throttle down and turn around when life starts to shimmy and shake. There is far too much fear as to what will happen before we hit the barrier. But just as Chuck discovered that, the air smoothed out and became peaceful when he pressed into the sky. Likewise, God will meet us with His peace and faithfulness in our obedience.

## You Have Been Good to Me

**GOD WILL MEET US WITH HIS PEACE AND FAITHFULNESS IN OUR OBEDIENCE.**

If anyone in the world today knows the name "Don Moen" as a worship leader, artist, or songwriter, likely the reason has something to do with Integrity Music. I spent twenty amazing years as a part of that company. While I had a few different titles over time, ending up as president of the music division, I am so grateful that God allowed me to be involved with such incredible people and to be a part of such a groundbreaking movement of worship.

Having a role in a fresh move of God that honored and blessed Him was such a privilege and an extraordinary experience. A Scripture verse we often quoted early on was Habakkuk 2:14: "Let the glory of the Lord cover the earth as the waters cover the sea" (author's paraphrase). I did indeed get the blessing of witnessing His glory all over the world. Not a day goes by that I am not grateful for getting a front-row seat to watch our great God move and make a way as only He can.

One of the songs I wrote during the season of stepping away from Integrity and into my own ministry on the platform that God built for me in that season was the song "I Believe There Is More":

> *You have been good to me*
> *You have been good to me*
> *You have been gracious*
> *You have been faithful*
> *Meeting my needs.*
> *Lord, it's so plain to see*
> *That You have been good to me*
> *I have been given so much*
> *I can't even begin to thank You.*
> *And still I believe there is more*
> *I believe there is more, I believe*
> *So open my hands to receive*
> *All that your love has in store*
> *Lord, I believe*[5]

Susan's vision that she sent to Laura did prove to be prophetic. During many years I have had the incredible privilege of leading thousands into the presence of God in power, praise, healing, and deliverance. The remarkably detailed part about that vision is that I have played before presidents and kings in several nations. We have witnessed that specific word come to pass. And then the final piece was that on many, many nights and all over the world, Laura was standing in the wings, being my full support. A few years ago, Laura found Susan's letter in one of her Bibles. Reading those words once again was so amazing and completely confirming.

I had to confess, "Maybe your sister is a prophet after all!"

Someone said to me recently, "There would never be a Don Moen without a Laura Moen." That statement is so true. My wife of forty-five-plus years has been a rock to me. She has never criticized, never judged, even when she should have, but has always supported me. Anyone who knows my wife knows the way she is and that these words are perfectly fitting. That's why I have always loved having her out on tour with me. Just as God said, "The two become one," when people see us together, they get to see the *real* Don Moen.

To God be the glory, great things He has done!

*chapter seven*

# THROUGH HIS MIRACLES

*"Most assuredly, I say to you, he who believes in Me, the works*
*that I do he will do also; and greater works than these he will*
*do, because I go to My Father. And whatever you ask in My*
*name, that I will do, that the Father may be glorified in the*
*Son. If you ask anything in My name, I will do it."*

—JOHN 14:12–14

When I attended Oral Roberts University, I once heard Brother Roberts teach, "Miracles are coming at you or going by you all the time. You just have to reach out and receive them." In today's digital age, when a computer can send an entire document through the air to your printer, there are obviously millions of pieces of information flying by us all the time. We can't see them, but we have come to know and believe they are indeed there.

The Bible says, "No eye has seen, no ear has heard, and no mind has imagined what God has prepared for those who love him" (1 Cor. 2:9–10 NLT). We can learn to keep our spirits tuned to the Holy Spirit's frequency so we can hear what He wants to reveal to us. We can *see* in the Spirit. We can *hear* in the Spirit. We can *pray* in the Spirit. We can *move* in the Spirit. We can sincerely ask God to reveal His miracles.

> WE CAN LEARN TO KEEP OUR SPIRITS TUNED TO THE HOLY SPIRIT'S FREQUENCY SO WE CAN HEAR WHAT HE WANTS TO REVEAL TO US.

One of the most amazing things about the Christian life is having opportunities to witness with our own eyes exactly what Jesus said in this passage. He tells us that we can and will take part in "the works that I do," as well as "greater works than these." How can this be? Because the same Spirit of the Father who dwelled in Jesus on earth now dwells in you and me, His adopted children. Just look at all the proactive verbs in these four verses. We can take part in the heavenly activity of God here on earth in our daily lives. His kingdom is here and we are citizens of heaven right now.

In this chapter I want to share some of the testimonies I have had the blessing and privilege to witness through the years, as I saw Jesus do exactly what He promised He would do.

## Healing in Hanoi

In the spring of 2011, I was invited to join renowned evangelist Luis Palau in Ho Chi Min City (Saigon) and Hanoi, Vietnam, to lead worship for the celebration of the one hundredth anniversary of the evangelical church in that nation. The communist government had miraculously agreed to let Luis come for a crusade. But upon arrival, they did everything they could to make life difficult for all of us involved. Just because God opens a door to a volatile place doesn't mean walking through it will be easy. Many times that door only leads to a spiritual battle.

The government forced the sponsors to change the venue at least twice, if not three times. Wanting to be good witnesses and obey Scripture by honoring the governing authorities, they worked hard to comply. Trying to get the word out on such short notice to such a massive audience as to where the crusade would be held was nearly impossible.

In Hanoi, they officially canceled the event even as hundreds of buses filled with people were arriving in the city from all over the nation. The church had effectively used the crusade and concert as an outreach opportunity inviting many non-Christians to come and hear the gospel. They had strategically assigned two believers to ride on each chartered bus traveling to the event to pray and be available for conversations that could lead to sharing Christ.

When the buses arrived at the stadium, government representatives were there to immediately turn them away. The people were met with the news that there would be no crusade and no concert. On one bus, there was an elderly woman who had a back injury and had suffered from being bent over for many years. Coming on the trip had been incredibly painful for her. As with the woman with the issue of blood who touched Jesus' robe, her condition made her desperate for any help. She had struggled in agony to make her way off the bus, only to be told to go back home. Horribly disappointed and frustrated, everyone turned to make their way back onto the bus. They knew better than to protest and create any pushback toward the government.

As everyone was seated once again, the two believers assigned to that particular bus stood in front of all the passengers and apologized for the event being canceled. Then they announced, "You came to hear the gospel tonight, so how many of you would still like to hear the good news of Jesus Christ?" Hands lifted all around the bus.

In the next few moments, the believers shared God's plan of salvation and led everyone in a prayer. After saying amen, the elderly lady with the bad back stood straight up! She was completely healed. The prayer had been for people who wanted to receive Christ, not for healing, not for injured backs, and not even for this particular woman. But when she simply asked Jesus into her life, her soul was saved for eternity and her body also was healed right at that moment.

"Greater works," just as Jesus promised.

The Palau organization heard this story from the local churches and was able to find out the woman's name and the village where she lived. They sent out a camera crew to document the story and interview her for confirmation of the miracle. When the crew arrived, they found a line of people almost a block long, waiting to hear her testimony. They had all known this woman for many years, knew she had been bent over in pain for a very long time, and wanted to hear for themselves the message of salvation that had saved and healed her.

In spite of the Vietnamese government trying to stop the preaching of the gospel, God made a way as people heard anyway, lives were changed, and the witness from the canceled crusade continued long after the event would have been held.

Jesus told the demon-possessed man whom He had just delivered and healed, "'Go home to your friends, and tell them what great things the Lord has done for you, and how He has had compassion on you.'

And he departed and began to proclaim in Decapolis all that Jesus had done for him; and all marveled" (Mark 5:18–20).

No government, no work of hell, and no effort of man can stop the gospel from going where God wills His message to go. He can turn the evils and ailments of this world into testimonies that change entire communities.

# Kneeling in the Bow

In 1976, we were traveling with Living Sound by ship from Southampton, England, to Cape Town, South Africa. We made this round-trip voyage three times in six years. Because it was too expensive to fly our entire team with all our musical and sound equipment, we negotiated with the Union-Castle Line to offer four concerts on board the ship—two for coach-class customers, one for first-class customers, and one for the crew. In return, they gave us discounted fares and shipped our gear for free.

With that many events planned, those trips weren't exactly a luxury cruise for us. We were all placed in the "stowage" area of the ship, which was well below the water line near the engine compartment. There were no windows or balconies and just enough room for two bunk beds per compartment. There was a sink in the room but the bathroom was down the hall. Traveling that distance took two weeks at sea with no stops until we reached Cape Town.

On the last night of the trip, we were given the opportunity to do a concert for the ship's crew at their bar called "The Pig & Whistle." The piano was wisely bolted to the floor so it couldn't move with the tossing of the vessel. As we approached Cape Town, we could see the huge waves through the open portals. The sensation felt like we were constantly going up and down in a six-floor elevator. After singing and sharing the gospel with the rowdy crew at their bar, we went back to our rooms for our last night at sea.

A few hours later at around 2:00 a.m., I was awakened by a knock at my door. Barely coherent, I staggered out of bed and answered. There stood one of the members of the crew I recognized as being in the crowd that night. I asked, "Hey, how can I help you? Is everything okay?" He wasted no time and said, "Yes, I want to become a Christian like you talked and sang about tonight."

With his confession, I was now wide awake and he and God had my full attention. I invited the man in to talk and pray.

He shook his head and said, "No. Not here. Follow me."

I quickly slipped on my shoes and filed in behind the man as he navigated through the narrow halls of the ship. We snaked around corners and through the crew's quarters, which I am confident was illegal since I had no clearance to be there. But he just kept going.

Finally, after climbing a flight of stairs, we came out onto the front deck of the ship, right at the bow where the anchor was held. I called out above the crashing of the waves, "I don't think this is a good idea! I'm not supposed to be out here!" The wind was howling and the fifty-foot-high "cape rollers," as the waves were called, looked massive from that vantage point.

He shouted out, "This is where I want to accept Christ!"

He knelt right there on the deck as I joined him, shouting in his ear, "Repeat this prayer after me! Dear Jesus, I believe You are the Son of God. You died on a cross for me. I am a sinner and I need a Savior. Please forgive my sins and come into my heart. Fill me with Your love. Fill me with Your Spirit. I choose to follow You. Thank You for hearing my prayer. Amen!"

We quickly left the area as he led me back through the crew's quarters to my room. He thanked me and we exchanged addresses.

Months later, I received a letter from the man. He said his decision to find me and follow Christ was the best choice he had ever made. He wrote, "When I prayed that prayer with you, there was an explosion that went off inside of me, and when it was over, all the bad was gone and only the good remained."

What a great way to express the transformative miracle of salvation, reminiscent of: "Old things have passed away; behold, all things have become new!" (2 Cor. 5:17). He closed out his letter with the assurance that he was growing spiritually and serving the Lord.

While to some it might seem odd, controversial, or even unacceptable for a Christian singing group to accept an invitation to sing at a bar, but when God opens a door to bring the light of the gospel into a dark world, we must obey. In such moments, we are simply following His example. Often, far more ministry occurs in places like the crew's bar below the deck of a ship than in the ship's ballroom full of guests. Jesus Himself said, "Those who are well have no need of a physician, but those who are sick. I did not come to call the righteous, but sinners, to repentance" (Mark 2:17)

—

I have so many stories from ministering around the world and incredible things that God has done, but, because I am still very active in international ministry today, I cannot afford to share details that might jeopardize future opportunities. I have had the privilege of sharing the gospel in places you would never believe it was possible. I have been invited into situations where people of all different religions

**OFTEN, FAR MORE MINISTRY OCCURS IN PLACES LIKE THE CREW'S BAR BELOW THE DECK OF A SHIP THAN IN THE SHIP'S BALLROOM FULL OF GUESTS.**

were in attendance and heard the truth about Christ. God is indeed a God of miracles.

There have been many times when word has gotten out into the American Christian community about international events I have agreed to do or places I have accepted to go and I have received criticism for taking part. But by the grace and favor of God, I have always been faithful to present the gospel and sing my songs of worship everywhere I go and have never—I repeat, *never*—been shut down, stopped, or censored anywhere in any nation. Jesus clearly commanded us to take the gospel to "all the nations" (Matthew 28:19). I have chosen to interpret His "all" to mean *all,* even when translating Greek into English.

In many nations and circumstances where I have presented the gospel and led in a prayer of salvation, altar calls have not been allowed. But the very real fact is that there may be no other Christians present to receive and pray for the people who would come forward. Therefore, I will not know until heaven how many may have accepted Christ over the years, but I do know the gospel has been allowed to be shared, many times through miraculous means, with those who have needed to hear.

I have been invited back multiple times to many places around the world that you would never suspect to be "gospel-friendly." God does indeed make a way where there *seems* to be no way.

In many of the dark places I am invited to go, I am often reminded of Romans 10:14–15: "How then shall they call on Him in whom they have not believed? And how shall they believe in Him of whom they have not heard? And how shall they hear without a preacher? And how shall they preach unless they are sent?"

One of the best examples of being bold for the sake of the gospel is found in Acts 4:

> Now when they saw the boldness of Peter and John, and perceived that they were uneducated and untrained men, they marveled. And they realized that they had been with Jesus. . . .
>
> So they called them and commanded them not to speak at all nor teach in the name of Jesus. But Peter and John answered and said to them, "Whether it is right in the sight of God to listen to you more than to God, you judge. For we cannot but speak the things which we have seen and heard." (vv. 13, 18–20)

While I do have a university education and am trained musically, that is not at all what I rely on when I am placed in circumstances to advance the gospel. Those aspects of my life may get me in the door, but once I'm in the room, the Holy Spirit takes over with the words to be spoken in each situation. As with Peter, John, and all the disciples, the Holy Spirit allows us to say, "For we cannot but speak the things which we have seen and heard."

## Concerts and Convoys

In April and May 1978, Living Sound toured for six weeks throughout what was then Rhodesia but is now Zimbabwe. The nation was in the middle of a war. Travel between cities was restricted because terrorists were notorious for stopping cars and killing the passengers. Because of the level of danger, the military stepped in and determined there would only be one trip each day from one city to the next for anyone, led by the army.

Anyone wanting to travel to another city had to meet at the edge of town at 6:00 a.m. and line up in the convoy. Three jeeps with anti-aircraft guns mounted on them were assigned to travel with each group. No matter how many vehicles there were, sometimes as many as thirty cars, there was one armored vehicle in the front, one in the middle, and one in the rear. Those days were long and extremely intense. There was constantly the possibility of finding ourselves in the middle of an attack.

On a previous trip, Prime Minister Ian Smith's son had experienced a dramatic conversion to Christ at one of our concerts. Knowing we had returned to his country, the prime minister invited our entire group to visit him at his residence. I remember being seated across from him, very aware what an honor it was to be in such a high-ranking official's home. Suddenly, one of the security guards came in and whispered something to Smith. The prime minister immediately called out, "Close the drapes! We're not leaving this room."

The prime minister then informed our group that someone had overpowered the guard at the security checkpoint outside his residence and had taken the guard's Uzi machine gun. The man shouted that he "was going to baptize Ian Smith in his own blood that afternoon."

Prime Minister Smith remained calm and continued with our conversation as if nothing had happened. He was obviously more accustomed to such threats than we were. But as each minute passed, I think I hunched lower and lower in my chair, expecting any moment for the huge picture windows around the room to be riddled and shattered with machine-gun fire—unless those drapes they had pulled were bulletproof.

I wanted to minimize myself as a target as much as possible. Although I was a part of the conversation, I had no recollection afterward of what was discussed because I was so distracted by fear. My sense of being blessed to be in that room was shrinking as well.

Finally, another man came in and told the prime minister that the gunman had been apprehended and "removed from the premises." While I wondered exactly what "removed" might have meant, we were all relieved the imminent threat was over. Now we were just back to the "norm" of the armed convoys.

Throughout Scripture and history, we see how the gospel affects the common man all the way to high government officials. Recorded in Acts 8, the Ethiopian whom Philip encountered was the treasurer for the queen, so God knew he would carry his new faith back to the palace, just as Prime Minister Smith's son had taken his conversion back to impact his father at such a critical time in the life of his nation.

When God saves someone, the ripple effects may vary in size, but the movement of Living Water always ends up touching countless lives. As Jesus said in our opening passage, "Greater works."

*chapter eight*

# THROUGH OUR TESTIMONY

In 1972, following a concert in Florida while I was out on a tour with Living Sound, I walked right through a glass door and cut some of the tendons in my right hand. While such an accident would affect anyone's day-to-day activities, being a guitar player, violinist, and piano player made this injury especially difficult. I had to leave the tour for six weeks to give the tendons a chance to heal before rejoining the group. While the cut was healed and my hand was much better, I still couldn't bend my little finger.

Shortly after I rejoined the tour, we were singing at the International Full Gospel Businessmen's Conference at the San Francisco Hilton Hotel. After we finished singing, we all sat down on the back row of the large meeting room where about two thousand people were gathered to hear the speaker. As he came to the stage to begin teaching, I heard him say, "There's a man here with a withered right hand. If you will lift it up to the Lord, you'll be healed."

I remember looking down at my finger and thinking, *Well, while I wouldn't necessarily call that "withered," the severed tendons sure are not working right.* So out of faith and obedience, I lifted my hand into the air just as he said. I was so far back in the room that I don't think anyone even saw me. Well, any human, I mean. After holding my hand in the air for a couple of minutes, I put it down and didn't feel anything. But I knew I had acted on the word given.

Later that night, after I had forgotten about raising my hand into the air, I began to feel a tremendous burning sensation in my right hand, feeling the strongest heat specifically in those tendons. By the next morning, my finger began to have more movement, and within three days, it was completely healed. Good as new!

I have often wondered, *What if I hadn't been in that room? What if I hadn't been listening to the message? What if I had decided not to lift my hand?* But I was, I did, and God did. I expressed faith and He healed me. While the accident put a hiatus on my playing and leading worship for a few weeks, God fully restored my ability to complete capacity with no hindrances. Except now I had a testimony for Him that I did not have before.

When God speaks, when He moves, we must embrace what He says and what He asks of us. We can easily allow our pride to get in His way. Being honest, I was embarrassed to lift my hand because I thought people would look at me and say, "Look! There's the man with the withered right hand!" In that moment, I had to make the decision to have fear of man or faith in God. Was I going to be concerned what my peers and a room of total strangers thought about me or focus on the fact that God wanted to heal my hand to better serve Him?

In 2 Kings 5, we read how Naaman resisted Elisha's word from God for his healing because he didn't want to wade into the dirty water of the Jordan River. But his entourage tried some psychology on him.

> And his servants came near and spoke to him, and said, "My father, if the prophet had told you to do something great, would you not

have done it? How much more then, when he says to you, 'Wash, and be clean'?" So he went down and dipped seven times in the Jordan, according to the saying of the man of God; and his flesh was restored like the flesh of a little child, and he was clean.

And he returned to the man of God, he and all his aides, and came and stood before him; and he said, "Indeed, now I know that there is no God in all the earth, except in Israel." (vv. 13–15)

But then we have examples of someone doing exactly what God asked, no matter who was watching. Jesus had entered the synagogue on the Sabbath. There was a man there with a withered hand and the Pharisees were watching Christ like hawks to see if He would "break the Law" and heal so they could accuse Him.

But He knew their thoughts, and said to the man who had the withered hand, "Arise and stand here." And he arose and stood. Then Jesus said to them, "I will ask you one thing: Is it lawful on the Sabbath to do good or to do evil, to save life or to destroy?" And when He had looked around at them all, He said to the man, "Stretch out your hand." And he did so, and his hand was restored as whole as the other. (Luke 6:8–10)

Look closely at the inside story of the man, aside from the Pharisees. "'Arise and stand here.' And he arose and stood." "'Stretch out your hand.' And he did so, and his hand was restored as whole as the other." While the teachers of the Law were splitting hairs over Jesus' actions, the man with the need was humbly submissive. The Pharisees walked away *exactly* the same, but the man who was healed was *never* the same.

We see throughout the New Testament that Jesus often used unconventional means to create miraculous outcomes. Remember the mud made from dirt and spit Jesus placed on the blind man's eyes? For miracles to occur in our lives, we have to be willing to be specifically obedient to God's requests.

> **FOR MIRACLES TO OCCUR IN OUR LIVES, WE HAVE TO BE WILLING TO BE SPECIFICALLY OBEDIENT TO GOD'S REQUESTS.**

I cannot know if I still would have been healed that day had I not raised my hand, but the reason I will never know is because I did! While we all constantly have great needs in our lives, we also must listen closely to God's instructions and exhibit faith in the way that He asks, even if it may be uncomfortable or feel strange at times.

## All the Time?

I was in the middle of a concert in Ohio when a lady stood up and interrupted me. I stopped singing and she asked if she could come up and share something. I agreed, which is always a bit risky. She began to share her testimony about not being able to sing my song "God Is Good All the Time." Ten years before, her teenage daughter had been killed in a car accident. Because of that tragedy, she just could not bring herself to say or sing those words anymore. How could God be good if He allowed her daughter to be taken from her in such a horrible manner at such a young age?

But that night by His covering of grace and mercy on her heart,

God gave this mother the ability to sing the words for the first time in many years. In spite of her situation, she was able to declare by faith that God *is* good all the time. And now the words had a new, even more profound meaning. Recognizing and confessing God's goodness in a situation that is anything but good does not make rational or logical sense. But we declare His goodness because it is true.

—

We received another testimony regarding this same song and we obtained permission to use it in the musical *God for Us*. The following is a mother's letter:

Dear Don,

You don't know us and we don't know you except through your praise and worship music. We understand you wrote the song, "God Is Good All the Time." This song has impacted my husband and me more than you realize. Our son, along with seven other young people and four adults, had traveled to a remote lake in the Canadian wilderness for a spiritual retreat and fishing trip. All week long they had been singing "God Is Good All the Time" as a theme song for the retreat.

Late one night after a wonderful time of fishing and fellowship around the campfire, they got into their boats to travel back to the cabin on the other side of the lake. A storm came up suddenly and, before they could paddle to shore, heavy waves and strong winds capsized their canoe and the two boats they had been in. As they were clinging to the boats in the icy 29-degree water, they sang the song they had been singing all week, "God Is Good All the Time," and committed their lives to their Creator. Out of the twelve, only four survived. Our son, Joseph, did not, but I know he was able to face death without fear.

In the musical, I continue after that testimony with, "My friend, perhaps you're in the midst of a storm that is threatening to capsize your marriage, your family, your health, or your finances. Listen, God hasn't forgotten you and He isn't against you. God is for you and He wants you to trust Him today in the midst of whatever storm you are facing. Let His peace come to you as we declare . . . by faith . . . God is good all the time."

I believe those young Christ followers began singing here on earth in that frigid lake but then finished their song in the warm light of the presence of their Savior. Rescue may not have come soon enough for some of them, but the ultimate rescue did occur eternally. No matter what life holds for us here on earth, eternal salvation is just one of the reasons that God is indeed good.

## The Deaf Will Hear

> NO MATTER WHAT LIFE HOLDS FOR US HERE ON EARTH, ETERNAL SALVATION IS JUST ONE OF THE REASONS THAT GOD IS INDEED GOOD.

I was in Boise, Idaho, leading worship at a church one Sunday morning. We were singing, "Holy, holy, holy, Lord God of power and might, heaven and earth are filled with Your glory. Hosanna, Hosanna in the highest!" The moment was one when you could palpably sense the presence of God in the room. I had my eyes closed as I was leading and when I opened them, almost everyone in the church was either on their knees or on their face before God. In that moment, a thirteen-year-old girl who had been deaf since birth ran to the front of the church completely healed! No one prayed for her. No one laid hands on her. Her ears were opened and she could hear! While we worshiped, God moved. While we praised Him, He healed.

On another occasion, I was at a large Baptist church in Fort Lauderdale, Florida, recording one of my Hosanna! Music projects called *Let Your Glory Fall*. We had a large orchestra and choir along with an amazing rhythm section that included Tom Brooks, Justo Almario, Paul Jackson Jr., Carl Albrecht, and Abraham Laboriel. We were in the middle of a dress rehearsal, which is

**WHILE WE WORSHIPED, GOD MOVED. WHILE WE PRAISED HIM, HE HEALED.**

almost always a hectic event. (I don't think there has ever been a time when I wished I had one day less of rehearsal before a big event.) We had just finished singing the title song "Let Your Glory Fall," and as is the norm, I had several people asking me questions about the arrangement, chords, and so on.

Suddenly there was a commotion in the choir. I looked back and saw two tenors in an animated discussion and thought to myself, *Great, another first in a Don Moen recording. Two tenors are about to get into a fight.* Understanding something serious was obviously going on, I shouted, "What's the problem?"

One of the men exclaimed, "I've been healed! I've been healed! My ear! I can hear! I can hear!"

He had been deaf in his left ear for at least twenty years. But in an instant, while we were singing, "Let Your Glory Fall," God opened his ear! Right in the middle of a crazy, chaotic dress rehearsal, his long-time prayer was answered. I wish I could say, "Yes, I sensed in my spirit that God was healing someone." But unfortunately, that wasn't the case. I actually thought the two guys were fighting. In spite of me, in spite of everything, God healed the man's ear while he worshiped. Years later when I was visiting the church again, I inquired about the man and was told his hearing was still normal, just as God had restored him that amazing day.

## Blessing in Brownsville

During the season at Integrity when I was flying to different churches every weekend to find new music coming out of great moves of God, Laura and I visited what came to be known as the "Brownsville Revival" or the "Pensacola Outpouring" at the renowned Brownsville Assembly of God Church in Pensacola, Florida. The movement of the Spirit there lasted for several years, beginning during a Father's Day worship service in 1995. As it was just about an hour's drive from our home in Mobile, we drove down to see the work for ourselves.

When I visited churches for these projects, I never wanted to be conspicuous, so I would usually sit in the back row to observe. But soon I saw a close friend who invited us to sit with him in the third row. The third row! That is not at all what I wanted to do. Walking up to the front, I saw several other people I knew.

Toward the end of the service, they asked for anyone who was there for the first time to come forward to receive prayer. I surprised

Laura by taking her hand and leading us to the front. Honestly, I even surprised myself. As many people were being prayed for, they would fall down. When we were prayed for, I waited but felt nothing. I didn't fall down. Neither did Laura. I felt really unspiritual. Everyone was looking at us and I imagined in the moment they were thinking, *Oh my, poor Don must not be very spiritual. He's just standing there.*

But then while I was feeling self-conscious and awkward, the Lord did speak to me as the people around us continued to pray. I heard Him quietly say, "Don, seek the Giver, not the gift. Don't seek an experience. Seek Me. Seek My face." I did, I have, and that's what I continue to do. While something did happen in the lives of many of my friends over the years at Brownsville, for that entire service I don't recall anything major for me other than that simple word of encouragement.

My point in sharing this story is that it is so important to embrace the move of God. He is constantly offering us opportunities to grow, increasing our testimony for Him and His glory for the purpose of touching the lives of others. Grab hold of whatever He is doing in your church or in the circles around you. While we may not understand everything that happens or doesn't happen, and like me you have probably seen some very weird things in the name of spirituality, maturing in the ways of God will never mean we have to accept some sort of heresy. Keep your eyes on Jesus. Receive all that He has especially for you. Expand your testimony of what Christ has done and is doing in and through you.

> "SEEK THE GIVER, NOT THE GIFT. DON'T SEEK AN EXPERIENCE. SEEK ME. SEEK MY FACE."

Psalm 22:3 states that God inhabits the praises of His people, that

He is enthroned on our praises. When we worship Him, we are building a throne for the King of kings and Lord of lords. When He comes to us in that visitation, He will heal, save, deliver, and provide for every need. While we may be more accustomed to hearing testimonies of evangelists and preachers facilitating healings and other miracles, in my own ministry I have witnessed many, many times God healing *as His people praise Him*. He comes in power as we praise, and as the Great I Am, He chooses what He does and when He does it. As John Wimber said, "The manifestation of the Spirit is not supposed to be the exception, it's supposed to be the norm."[3]

> **GOD COMES IN POWER AS WE PRAISE, AND AS THE GREAT I AM, HE CHOOSES WHAT HE DOES.**

I will praise You, O Lord, with my whole heart;
I will tell of all Your marvelous works.

(PSALM 9:1)

Don with his brother and sisters, 1958.
From left to right: Diane, Wendy, Don, and Denny.

High school photo, 1964.

Living Sound team, 1972.

Singing and playing
guitar with Living Sound,
March 1972, Trinidad.

Playing electric guitar
with Living Sound.
(One of my many guitars!)

Rhodesia, 1972, after
one of our concerts
with Living Sound.

Laura and Don, 1972,
Victoria Falls, Rhodesia.

Playing my 1963 Fender jazz bass
guitar with Living Sound, 1972.
(I sold this guitar in South
Africa to buy a diamond for
Laura in April 1973.)

Just married, May 19, 1973,
Minneapolis, Minnesota.

John's birth on the bathroom floor, March 17, 1990. From left to right: Don (holding Rachel and Michael), Laura (holding John), and Melissa.

Family photo at the Gulf Coast, September 1994. From left to right: Rachel, Melissa, John, Don (holding James), Laura, and Michael.

Having fun with Manny Pacquiao, November 2013, before my concert in General Santos City, Philippines.

With Manny and Jinkee Pacquiao at their home, November 2013, General Santos City, Philippines.

Johnson Beach, Florida, August 2016.
From left to right: James, Melissa, Jesse, Laura (holding Hank),
Don (holding Stella), Caylin, Michael, John, Sarah (holding Luke).

Celebrating our forty-fifth wedding anniversary,
May 19, 2018, Fisher's Seafood Restaurant on the Gulf Coast.

Lagos, Nigeria, 2008.

On tour with my friend
Lenny LeBlanc.

Leading worship in Africa.

On tour. From left to right: Don
Moen (on keyboard), Jason Foster
Rachel Robinson, and Tom Lane.

love ending with the fiddle on "God Is Good All the Time."

New Year's Eve 2014, Toronto.

Star Performing Arts Center, Singapore.

Royal Seed Home, Accra, Ghana.

*chapter nine*

# THROUGH LIFE'S INTERRUPTIONS

The very first time I led people in worship was in January 1983 in Woodward, Oklahoma. But there was just one problem. Snow. Everything, including the roads, was covered in snow. In the Northeast or upper Midwest, that is just normal fare for those folks, but that is not the case in Oklahoma. People stay home in weather like that. In spite of the inclement conditions, twenty-five faithful showed up that night and we had almost as many, about twenty people, onstage.

Seated at the piano nestled in the back with the band, I had hired five singers to be out front and lead that night. But I had set up a microphone for me just in case I decided to share with the audience. At the end of the scheduled set, I felt a strong sense that there was something more God wanted to do. It took a big step of faith for me as I spoke into the mic with a shaky voice, "Let's all sing that song one more time," as I led everyone back into the classic worship anthem "I Exalt Thee."

As everyone began singing, we experienced one of those holy moments when the Spirit starts sweeping through the room—wall to wall and floor to ceiling. The spiritual realm converged with the physical world and we could literally feel it. What began to happen wasn't because of my nervous voice or piano playing, which at that point was mediocre at best, but rather because I made the choice to step out into what God had called me to do. People followed me as we dove deeper into His presence.

That was my very first adventure of leading God's people to His throne, and I have never stopped since that night. God interrupted my life on that snowy evening in the presence of a handful of good, godly people by creating something in my spirit that allowed me to have a taste of heaven. I was like a beggar who got word of a banquet. I wanted others who were starving to find the feast too. I am always amazed and energized any and every time I sit down at a piano and watch God make a way with His people in this broken world.

Someone once told me, "Don, your piano is your pulpit. Don't be intimidated by great preachers. You do what God has called you to do. When you sit at the piano and lead worship, you will experience His favor." I have never forgotten that word of empowerment and affirmation to lean into and trust what the Father has placed in my hands and heart for His kingdom.

In your own life, there either has been or will be your own version of a holy moment like I had in Oklahoma. We must pay attention and watch for those times when God reveals His calling for us by His interruptions.

———

In the 1981 Academy Award–winning film *Chariots of Fire* (the true story of Eric Liddell, the Scotsman who ran in the 1924 Olympics), there is a scene where his sister is expressing her deep concern to him that his competitive running is pulling him away from their commitment to go to China together as missionaries. Eric looks deep into her eyes and tells his sister, "I believe God made me for a purpose, but He also made me fast. And when I run, I feel His pleasure."[4] He did run in the Olympics but also went on to serve the Lord in China.

One of the most beautiful yet amazing ways that we know we are fulfilling our purpose and tapping into the heart of God is when we "feel His pleasure," as Liddell explained to his sister. Knowing deep down that the activity in which you are engaged is a gift from your Creator and why He has placed you on this planet. That gift, that calling, is a part of you that just feels supernatural and you know when you connect with the passion that it is not about you but rather about God touching and reaching others through you.

## "Excuse Me, Don"

I was leading worship at Pastor Jack Hayford's Church on the Way in California when he came up to the stage after one of my songs and said, "Don, I don't know if this is Jack Hayford or the Holy Spirit, but I feel that we are supposed to take a few minutes and pray for those who are sick. Does that bear witness with anyone here?" As I continued to play quietly and lead in worship, Pastor Hayford came to the front as about two hundred people eventually walked to the altar for prayer.

I've always been so impressed by the way Pastor Jack handled that situation and I learned so much from him in other moments like that one. He could have adamantly stated, "God is telling me that we're supposed to pray for those who are sick." With his credibility and authority, no one would have questioned him. But instead he very humbly shared, "I don't know if this is Jack Hayford or the Holy Spirit."

Wow! He instantly had my attention. I wish more Christian leaders would present their promptings that way, because that's exactly how I feel most of the time. *Is this thought I have right now from God, or is it just the pizza I ate last night?*

The reason that I had absolutely no problem with Pastor Jack "interrupting" my concert was because I *know* he hears from God. I trust his walk with Christ and his many years of successfully ushering the kingdom onto the earth through his ministry.

Throughout my career, I have come to love when the Holy Spirit disrupts and intervenes in the plans of man, including *this* man. Sometimes the most important part of my worship concerts is what happens in between the songs as He speaks. Listening intently for the Father's voice in any setting or situation is a vital part of our relationship with Him.

In my friend Bruce Wilkinson's book *You Were Born for This: Seven Keys to a Life of Predictable Miracles*, he talks about "God's nudges," describing how one minute we can be thinking about one thing, then seemingly out of the blue, a thought comes for which we have no explanation. Bruce encourages us to respond when God nudges.[5]

> LISTENING INTENTLY FOR THE FATHER'S VOICE IN ANY SETTING OR SITUATION IS A VITAL PART OF OUR RELATIONSHIP WITH HIM.

But how can we identify those moments when they come? We need to *anticipate* His involvement in our lives and *expect* Him to show up, whether in a worship service or a simple lunch meeting with a friend. That's why I love the story of Jesus interrupting the disciples' conversation on the Emmaus Road, recorded in Luke 24.

Two of Jesus' disciples, evidently not any of the original twelve, had left Jerusalem when they found out that His body was missing from the tomb. Disappointed and disillusioned, they left, thinking the story was over. Jesus must have really loved these guys because He came after them to reveal why they needed to go back to join the others.

Christ walked up to them and asked, basically, "What's up, guys? What are you talking about?" For whatever reason, they did not recognize Him. They got a bit edgy that this apparent stranger would even ask such a question after what they had been through. Finally, they explained to Him their take on Jesus and what happened. Let's look at what occurred next.

> And beginning with Moses and all the Prophets, he explained to them what was said in all the Scriptures concerning himself. . . .
>
> When he was at the table with them, he took bread, gave thanks, broke it and began to give it to them. Then their eyes were opened and they recognized him, and he disappeared from their sight. They asked each other, "Were not our hearts burning within us while he talked with us on the road and opened the Scriptures to us?"
>
> They got up and returned at once to Jerusalem. (Luke 24:27, 30–33 NIV)

Imagine for a moment having Jesus tell you the story of the Bible from Moses through the Prophets, connecting all the dots straight to Him! What an amazing intrusion that changed those men's lives forever. God has those same types of life interruptions planned for us.

# I Will Sing

I was scheduled to record a new project for Integrity. There's nothing quite like seeing a recording date on a calendar to force your creativity, so I made the decision to go away alone to write the music. I rented a beach cottage for five days. Day one began and I worked hard to get something solid down on paper. But nothing came. Day two. Nothing. As the days counted down, my fear and frustration only grew. Suffering from a horrible case of writer's block, I prayed and attempted to write but to no avail.

I began to get angry. I started feeling like God had let me down. After all, I had scheduled the time, spent good money, gone away, and gotten alone, so where was He? He knew exactly why I had carved out those five days, so why couldn't He cooperate with *my* plans? I had prayed and prayed for Him to speak. But I didn't hear God once.

At the end of day five, I packed up the car and started driving home. I put my pen and legal pad beside me in the seat, just in case. As I drove alone, I decided I was going to take a chance and get really honest with God. Like *very* honest. Back at the beach, I had prayed a lot of pretty prayers, but now I was just going to speak my mind.

I began, "Lord, You seem so far away. A million miles or more, it feels today." I paused a moment and when lightning didn't strike my car, I continued, "And though I haven't lost my faith, I must confess right now that it's hard for me to pray." I thought to myself, *Hey, this kind of sounds like it could be a song lyric.* I kept going: "But I don't know what to say and I don't know where to start, but as You give the grace, with all that is in my heart, I will sing, I will praise. Even in my darkest hour through the sorrow and the pain, I will sing and I will praise. I lift my hands to honor You, because Your Word is true, I will sing."[9]

The five-day drought came to an end on the way home—after I had surrendered, given up, and gotten honest. Right when I *least* expected and not when I wanted. What I needed came when I got real with God. The state of my mind and heart prompted an authentic prayer that became the song I needed to write. By the time I arrived back at my house, I had written down all the lyrics. I went directly to my piano and played the melody almost exactly as you still hear the song today. (Oh, how I wish every song came together that fast!)

But then as I studied the lyrics, I said to God and myself, "Wait! I can't record *that*. 'Lord, You seem so far away? A million miles or more, it feels today?' I can't possibly say those words in a song!" So I took the safe route and decided to keep "I Will Sing" off my completed list for the time being. After all, I didn't want people to think I had issues, especially with God.

Eventually, I played the song for Laura. While she liked the honesty of the words, I still struggled. Tommy Coomes, an artist friend, came by and I played it for him. He loved the lyrics, saying they were honest and profound. So I slowly expanded the circle of people to listen and get their reactions. Person after person agreed with Laura and Tommy. Everyone loved the transparency of the message and felt the song needed to be shared.

The truth is we are more often in this spiritual state than we want to admit, which is exactly why people related to the words. Several people said, "Thank you for being honest, Don. Everyone is afraid to say those words." The song ended up being the title of the project. The cover was a photo from the dress rehearsal where God's presence overwhelmed us all. (Yes, yet another rehearsal where the Spirit showed up!) I'll admit that it's not the most flattering shot, with tears running down my face, but the emotion was real and expressed what so many people feel: "Even in my darkest hour, through the sorrow and the pain, I will sing, and I will praise."

# Paralyzing Panic

In 1999, before a crowd of about twelve thousand in the Hong Kong Coliseum, right in the middle of the program, I suddenly became very dizzy and disoriented. I began to sweat and feel very strange. My chest was tight and heavy. The only conclusion that I could come to was I must be having a heart attack. I thought I was dying. One moment I was fine. The next I was just trying to catch my breath and make the room stop spinning.

I had been smiling, standing, holding a microphone, leading the huge crowd in praise, but when that horrible wave from the inside hit me, I had to quickly sit back down at the piano. One of the singers standing closest to me realized something was not right. She asked, obviously concerned, "Don, what is wrong?" While I was working hard to stay focused, I was starting to miss the lyrics in the song.

Legendary bassist Abraham Laboriel was with me that night. Just as the song ended and I was trying to regain my composure to figure out what to do, he walked over with his electric bass around his neck and whispered in my ear, "Don, I think God wants you to sing a blessing over Hong Kong." Without explaining the horrible feelings and physical manifestations I was having, I told him, "No, I think you are supposed to, Abraham."

Being a man of God and a professional, Abe strolled up to the mic at the front of the stage and began to play one of his signature funky bass lines as only he can. As the crowd began to clap in rhythm to his groove, Abe sang an impromptu blessing over Hong Kong.

While all eyes were on Abe, I kept hearing a voice say to me, "You're going to die on this stage tonight." The threat just played on repeat in my mind. But somehow I managed to struggle through the evening and finish out the event without the audience realizing anything.

That night back at the hotel I said to Laura, "Babe, I think something is wrong with me." I told her what I had experienced and we talked it out. While I felt much better, the experience had certainly shaken me. But the next day on a flight from Hong Kong to Jakarta, I began to have the exact same feelings and symptoms. I suddenly felt claustrophobic and trapped. The plane seemed to shrink and I felt the walls closing in on me. I wanted nothing more than to get out of that cramped airplane seat, but of course, I couldn't. At thirty thousand feet traveling at 550 miles per hour, the options for freedom are limited or lethal.

When we arrived in Jakarta, I told our host that I needed to see a doctor as soon as possible, and they had someone meet me in my hotel room. While looking me over, and after hearing my story of the concert and plane ride, the doctor said he was going to call an ambulance. He was concerned I either had or was having a heart attack. He wanted to order a medical flight to take me to Singapore for heart surgery. And, of course, hearing that news only made my condition worse. At that point in the trip, I had four more concerts left to do, including a live recording scheduled in Singapore. I refused the flight and told the doctor I just wanted to get to a local hospital.

They rushed me to the nearest location as fast as Jakarta rush-hour traffic would allow. After completing several tests, the doctor informed me that my heart was fine. He went on to say I was obviously extremely fatigued. But then his next words completely threw me: "Mr. Moen, I believe the two episodes you experienced were panic attacks."

"Panic attacks?" I responded. While I had heard the term, I honestly had no idea what they were. The doctor went on to explain the perfect storm of ongoing physical, mental, and emotional trauma and what can occur in the mind and body as a result. Plus I also connected the spiritual element of hearing the taunting voice tell me, "You are going to die on this stage tonight," almost simultaneously coupled with Abe Laboriel's sense that I needed to sing a blessing over the city. The spiritual forces of darkness present there obviously did not want me singing God's blessing over the city.

The doctor told me I needed to remove all stress from my life and just rest. (Yeah, right! In the middle of a tour!) I told him I couldn't possibly cancel, so he responded with, "Okay, but no more interviews!" He then wrote out a prescription that was supposed to calm me down. I left the hospital and, being honest, within about four hours I was back on the original schedule. I did manage to finish out the tour and return home with only a few minor issues.

A few weeks later, I was in Los Angeles, California, right in the middle of one of those infamous dead-stop, stand-still, six-lane traffic jams on the 405. Frustrated and hemmed in among all those cars with no means of escape, just like in the plane that day, what I now knew to be another panic attack began. If you have never experienced one of these meltdowns, let me just tell you, you wouldn't wish them on your worst enemy.

I immediately called my doctor at home in Mobile. I told him about Hong Kong and Jakarta and then asked what was happening to me. He told me to come see him as soon as possible. When I got back home and went to my appointment, he asked me to tell him the entire story of this new malady in my life. I described the tremendous financial stress of keeping the cash flowing for my band and concert events, about the earthquake that had canceled two sold-out shows in Taiwan that worsened the financial situation, and then about my mother's recent death from Alzheimer's.

He looked at me with that stern face that only a veteran doctor can pull off and said, "You have several major issues that you have chosen *not* to deal with, and until you do, your mind and body will not cooperate with your fast-paced lifestyle."

He had my full attention.

From that experience, I saw firsthand how paralyzing fear and anxiety could be. God showed me in that season that I am not super-human, how I must take everything to Him and receive all the help I can get. Sweeping grief and pain under the rug while acting like the stress was not consuming me, wasn't helping anyone.

First Peter 5:7 says, "Cast all your anxiety on him because he cares for you" (NIV). The word *cast* isn't like a gentle handing off, but more the picture of catapulting or throwing your burdens and worries on Christ, allowing Him to take them and replace them with His peace. That certainly is not easy for us self-reliant creatures, but He invites us to trust Him with the details of our lives.

God doesn't cause things like depression and anxiety, but He obviously allows them to get through to us to get our attention. Our lives become interrupted by our inability to deal with burdens, which He never designed us to shoulder alone.

# Prayer and the Presence of Evil

Over the course of my career, I have experienced spiritual warfare and the presence of evil all over the world. Whenever I get invited to a country, I always encounter some type of spiritual warfare during the first visit. I associate this phenomenon with landing at the beaches at Normandy on D-Day. The battle will be the strongest at the initial entry point. There will always be a great resistance from the enemy to stop a team of people from coming in to worship God, especially if that nation is not accustomed to public Christian events. These events create a direct assault on the enemy's strongholds in that place.

**GOD DOESN'T CAUSE THINGS LIKE DEPRESSION AND ANXIETY, BUT HE OBVIOUSLY ALLOWS THEM TO GET THROUGH TO US TO GET OUR ATTENTION.**

For example, in Taipei, Taiwan, we were scheduled to play at an outdoor park with about three thousand people in attendance. The organizers had placed us strategically where they thought we could have the highest impact on the locals. Before the event started, a dog kept running up to the middle center area in front of the stage and frantically barking nonstop, obviously attempting to warn us of *something*. But nothing was visible to any of us that would indicate what the dog was sensing. After a while someone came to remove the animal from the park. But they must not have taken him very far away because soon he ran right back to that same spot, barking again. Even when they came to take him away one last time, the dog fixed his attention on the stage, fighting his best to turn around. He never stopped barking until he was well out of sight.

What occurred during the concert may have been a clue as to what was upsetting the dog. Suddenly, during an up-tempo praise song, a man came running down the aisle. At first I thought he was just an exuberant worshiper. But as he got to the front of the stage, he jumped about eight feet in the air and landed flat-footed right in front of where I was seated at the piano. I had never before witnessed what appeared to be some kind of superhuman strength. When I saw the evil in his eyes, I knew I was in trouble as he lunged toward me.

Let me hit the pause button to freeze-frame your mental visual image for a moment and rewind to a night at home before I left on that trip. During a very sound sleep, I had a dream that I was attacked onstage at a concert and the man killed me. Obviously, that was a frightening experience to awaken from. I was not at all certain if the dream was a warning from God or a threat from Satan or both. But now the scene was being played out exactly as I had seen and my nightmare was suddenly becoming reality.

I had decided not to tell Laura about the dream. It didn't seem like the kind of thing you should share with your wife as you are about to leave for a trip while she's left behind with five small children.

"Goodbye, honey. Oh, and by the way, I had a dream that I was going to be attacked and killed on this trip."

I confidentially shared the details with just one person at Integrity and asked him to pray specifically for divine protection. I had given the situation to the Lord and prayed for His shield to surround me.

> The God of my strength, in whom I will trust;
> My shield and the horn of my salvation,

My stronghold and my refuge;

My Savior, You save me from violence.

(2 SAMUEL 22:3)

All right, now that you know the backstory, let's hit play and restart the action. As the man lunged at me, his feet literally came out from under him like some invisible wrestler's tripping move had been performed. He landed facedown on the stage right by my piano, within a foot of me. Security guards ran out from both sides of the stage and managed to subdue him before he could stand and try again. As they took him away, he told the guards he had heard voices that told him very specifically: "Kill Don Moen."

At the point the man charged the stage, we were only on our third song. We were all obviously shaken up but we still had the concert to finish. After having my life threatened, I went back out and led the people in worship. For the rest of the evening, I decided to take an I-dare-you approach by standing right at the front center of the stage. And that concert was the first of a two-night booking, so we had to come back the next evening to the very same park. By the grace of God, nothing else happened.

The Lord knew the spiritual battle being readied against me and had warned me in the dream. I prayed, along with my band and the event organizers, agreeing and submitting to our Stronghold and Refuge who, once again, rescued me from the threats of darkness. There are many other stories about times we have seen His hand at work on our behalf as we have traveled throughout the world. I clearly know these acts of warfare are never really about me but about the threat of the gospel and the worship of the one true God who is a clear and present danger to Satan.

Scriptures like the one below weren't just for the day of the prophets, nor are they just for the super-Christian today; they are for people like you and me. I invite you to claim these verses in your life for your own battles:

"In righteousness you shall be established;
You shall be far from oppression, for you shall not fear;
And from terror, for it shall not come near you.
Indeed they shall surely assemble, but not because of Me.
Whoever assembles against you shall fall for your sake.

"Behold, I have created the blacksmith
Who blows the coals in the fire,
Who brings forth an instrument for his work;
And I have created the spoiler to destroy.
No weapon formed against you shall prosper,
And every tongue which rises against you in judgment
You shall condemn.
This is the heritage of the servants of the Lord,
And their righteousness is from Me,"
Says the Lord.

(Isaiah 54:14–17)

*chapter ten*

# THROUGH OUR
# COOPERATION WITH HIM

In 2008 I was invited to sing in Lagos, Nigeria, at an event called "The Experience." Today, this event is the largest Christian music festival in Africa and one of the largest in the world. In 2017, more than seven hundred thousand people attended. After my first experience in West Africa, specifically Ghana, I wasn't necessarily excited about going back. Ron Kenoly, Israel Houghton, and Pastor Paul Adefarasin, who was putting on the event, all called me. They assured me the event was going to be better than what I had experienced there the previous year. (I've been back to Ghana many times and have had great experiences there. Our charity, Don Moen & Friends, supports about two hundred children there every year.)

When I asked who else was going to be at the event, it was like a "who's who" of gospel music: CeCe Winans, Marvin Winans, Fred Hammond, Donnie McClurkin, Tye Tribbett, Kirk Franklin, Mary Mary, Israel and New Breed, Ron Kenoly, and many more. The artists were bringing their entire bands. There was simply no way I could hope to outperform or outdo the incredible musicianship of the other artists, so I chose to scale back by just bringing Rachel, my alto singer, and Tom, my tenor, who also played acoustic guitar.

Upon arrival and after I heard the stellar production of the other artists, I knew I had made a terrible mistake by not bringing my full band with me. When my set time came, I walked out to my piano, sat down, and began to play an intro to one of my songs to be sure everything was working. As soon as my first chord came through the huge sound system, I heard about two hundred thousand people begin singing one of my songs. So I decided to go with it, keep playing, and just follow them.

When we ended that song, the other side of the massive crowd started singing another of my songs. I followed them too. That was the way my entire concert went. I accompanied the Nigerian masses who had gathered there as they worshiped God through my music. Hearing hundreds of thousands of people singing along with every word was surprising, humbling, and absolutely beautiful. Pure heaven. While I had never been to Nigeria, my music obviously had been there before me.

I remember seeing CeCe and Marvin Winans standing in the wings, watching me and also watching the crowd. When I finished my set and walked off, CeCe said to me, teasingly, "*Who* are you?! Everybody knows your songs and you've never been here before!"

An embarrassing moment for me on that trip was when all the artists were picked up at the airport after arriving in Lagos. We were all loaded into cars to go to the hotel. As we were driving down the road, there was a huge billboard emblazoned with my picture and "Don Moen at The Experience." The other artists were pictured below me. As we drove past that sign, I sank down as far as I could in the seat of the car, embarrassed to see my image so much bigger than so many legendary artists. To this day when I run into those friends, we still laugh about that billboard and my embarrassment.

I had no idea that my music was so well known in Nigeria. I guess you could say that I found out the good way. Since that event years ago, I have been back more than twenty times. But just as it had been with the pastor at the church dedication service in New York, the Experience organizers didn't want just gospel music—they wanted worship. Praise was the common denominator that crossed racial, cultural, generational, and denominational boundaries and brought people together under the same banner—Jesus.

Any question I had about why I was there vanished as the people sang their hearts out toward heaven. Worship broke down barriers and borders, even in music genres. The simplicity of my songs had reached into the hearts of that nation long before I ever arrived. The music had gone before me and paved the path. God had once again made a way to the hearts of people through power and praise. Psalm 40:3 strikes again!

—

A similar situation occurred my first time in the Philippines. On that particular trip, I had my full band with me. As we arrived at the airport, I looked out of the plane window and saw reporters, photographers, and TV cameras with crowds of people on the tarmac, waiting to meet someone who was obviously on our plane. I said to Carl, my drummer, "Someone famous must be on our flight." Then I saw a huge poster through the window in the terminal with my name and picture and realized the crowd was waiting on me. I thought, *You have got to be kidding?!* But once again, my songs had arrived before me.

I shared these stories with you because I don't have the vocal chops of my Christian music counterparts. My range is normal. My level of talent is okay. I cannot rely on vocal acrobatics for one simple reason: I don't have any. But all these facts cause me to fully rely on the Spirit of God when I lead worship. If He doesn't show up, I am sunk and so is my music. At events when I stop to consider the other singers I'm sharing the stage with, many of them my heroes, I think, *I know why that artist is here, and that band, but why in the world am I here?*

In one ear, I hear a voice that says, "Don, you'd better dial up this performance because people are going to realize that you just are not good enough." But then I hear a different voice whisper in my other ear, "Just be Don Moen and use the talents I gave you. I'll work through you. Just give Me your best tonight."

I often work with a well-known artist, Lenny LeBlanc. When Lenny begins to sing, I always think, *How can this guy be so good?* But then God tells me I'm not supposed to be Lenny, I'm supposed to be me.

I have found that when your greatest *temptation* is to compete, then the worst *decision* you can make is to compete. I decided many years ago that since I really can't be competitive with other Christian artists, then I won't, and I don't. They are my fellow brothers and sisters in Christ serving Him with their gifts. I am only responsible for my own. No matter who else is on the platform or how great anyone else is shouldn't matter to me. My job description is simply to *cooperate* with God, not *compete* with others.

> **MY JOB DESCRIPTION IS SIMPLY TO *COOPERATE* WITH GOD, NOT *COMPETE* WITH OTHERS.**

I tell young artists all the time, "Be yourself, because everyone else is taken." This truth goes for pastors and ministers too. In this day and age of the internet, YouTube, streaming, TV, and social media, it is so easy to see amazing preachers and Christian singers and musicians anytime, anywhere. The temptation is always there to try to duplicate or replicate what you have seen and heard. But that doesn't work, especially in the kingdom of God. Be authentic. Be real. Be yourself. When you do, you'll find that God will give you His cloak of authority and wrap it around you (Isaiah 61:10). He will never anoint who *you want to be*, but He anoints who you *are*!

Jesus' parables taught countercultural principles to His followers when He lived on earth, as well as to us today. While in our self-centeredness we want to promote ourselves, He calls us to passionately pursue Him, allowing His Spirit to decide where we are placed in life's line-up.

When Jesus noticed how guests picked the places of honor at the table, He told them this parable:

> **HE WILL NEVER ANOINT WHO *YOU WANT TO BE*, BUT HE ANOINTS WHO YOU *ARE*!**

"When someone invites you to a wedding feast, do not take the place of honor, for a person more distinguished than you may have been invited. If so, the host who invited both of you will come and say to you, 'Give this person your seat.' Then, humiliated, you will have to take the least important place. But when you are invited, take the lowest place, so that when your host comes, he will say to you, 'Friend, move up to a better place.' Then you will be honored in the presence of all the other guests. For all those who exalt themselves will be humbled, and those who humble themselves will be exalted." (Luke 14:8–11 NIV)

# From Alaska to Immanuel

In June 1987, when I had gone back to writing some advertising jingle packages to subsidize our budget, I saw that the "real money" was being made by the salesmen selling my jingles to the banking and automotive industries. I figured I could do that as well as any of those guys, so I prayed about it. I honestly thought I heard the Lord say to me, "If you go to Alaska to sell advertising campaigns, you'll make twenty thousand dollars." We really needed the money since I had left Terry Law's ministry a year before and hadn't had a steady paycheck since. I was doing everything I could do to make a living for my family of four at the time.

I mapped out the trip, told Laura and the kids goodbye, and left to seek my fortune. The bottom line is I spent two weeks up there, going to four cities, and nothing happened. And I mean nothing. I was spending money to be there and not making a dime. I worked from sunup to sundown, which in Alaska in June is about twenty-two hours a day. I visited almost every bank and car dealership I could find from Fairbanks to Anchorage to Juneau to the North Pole. (Yes, there really is a town named North Pole, Alaska. I know because I was told no there!) I pitched many business owners some incredible new advertising campaigns such as "We're Good for You and Fairbanks Too" and "We're the Bank of a Lifetime." I'm sure you are moved by those titles, right?

After two solid weeks of making pitches, I was completely exhausted and out of money with not one sale to show for all my work. Discouraged, I flew back to see a friend, Dale, who lived in Juneau. He took me in his floatplane to go fishing at his lodge. When we landed, there was a message on his ship-to-shore radio that said I needed to get back to Anchorage right away for a meeting the next morning with a car dealership. Evidently, they were ready to buy a campaign.

Without ever touching a fishing pole, we barely got the plane back into the water because the tide had started to go out. Dale dropped me off in Juneau, and I caught the last flight up to Anchorage that night. I thought to myself, *This entire trip is all about this one sale, right here in the eleventh hour.*

First thing the next morning, I was up and at the dealership. Everything seemed to be going well as I was sitting in the owner's office while he looked over the papers, about to sign a thirty-five-thousand-dollar deal for a new ad campaign with original jingles by Don Moen. In a matter of minutes, this trip was about to make perfect sense and find redemption. But then one of the strangest encounters I have ever had in my entire life occurred.

Just as he was about to sign on the dotted line, he looked up at me and shouted, "You are a manipulator of people!" Everything changed in a heartbeat. I had no idea what happened. To this day, I still don't know what happened. All I know was that he went from being a really nice guy to being a tyrant who wanted me thrown out of his dealership.

Two guys who looked like bar bouncers grabbed me by both arms, literally carrying and dragging me out of the office. They brought me through the showroom where customers who had been looking at new cars were now staring at me. They threw me out of the dealership doors. I was speechless. That was one of those surreal moments when your mind tries desperately to play catch-up to what just happened to your body.

I got into my car and drove back to the hotel I had just left an hour before, but the room had already been sold for that night. The day was June 21, 1987, also known as summer solstice, the longest night of the year as well as the longest party of the year in Alaska. There were no more flights back to Juneau that night, but I did manage to find the last room available in Anchorage at a not-so-nice place called the Eagles Nest Motel.

Once in the room, I took out my cassette recorder I had used to play the jingles for the car dealers and put in a teaching tape by Reverend Charles Capps entitled "How to Build Up the Human Spirit." And boy did I need to hear that! I had left Laura and the kids in Tulsa two weeks before and flown all the way to Alaska because I thought I heard the Lord say that I would *make* twenty thousand dollars. But in that very lonely and discouraging moment, I came to realize I had missed God's message by just one word. He didn't say I would *make* that much money, but *lose* it if I went. I had heard what I wanted to hear. He wasn't giving me permission to go, but rather trying to protect me from going.

I didn't know what I was going to do. How would I tell Laura that we were now horribly in debt because of my foolish decision? I was now officially at the bottom, trying to see which way was up, and was so very discouraged.

Around midnight, as I was lying in bed with my ear next to the portable cassette player, I heard the door to the room next to me open with a thud, accompanied by laughter, rustling, and grunting from a couple who obviously had too much to drink. The walls were paper-thin so, unfortunately, I was hearing every sound as they jumped onto the bed. I thought to myself, *How much worse can this night get?* as I pushed the tape player even closer to my ear. Let's just say that even with the pillow over my head and Reverend Capps teaching the Word as loud as I could turn him up, I could still hear far more than I wanted from next door for much too long.

That was indeed the low point of my life. The next day, I flew to Juneau to say goodbye to my friend Dale before heading home with the bad news. As I walked through his office looking over his bookshelves, one title caught my attention: *The Tabernacle of Moses.* I took the book down from the shelf and began to skim through the pages. Referencing Hebrews 9, one chapter described all the articles of furniture in the tabernacle of Moses and explained how they were a shadow or symbol of how we are to come into God's presence. Something about that message strongly connected with my spirit.

Through those words, I got the idea to write a musical that would take the audience on a journey from the outer courts of the temple, through the inner courts, and finally into the Holy of Holies. After I returned home from Alaska, from July to December I wrote all the songs needed for the musical. Integrity produced and released *God with Us* in 1993. The project became one of the all-time bestselling Christian musicals, for which I received a Dove Award.

When I talk about the fiasco of that trip and how I missed God's will, Laura always reminds me that I eventually made far more in royalties from the musical inspired by the book I found on the last day of my trip than I lost in expenses during those two weeks. Out of being rejected and verbally assaulted in Alaska, I ended up writing songs about the God who walks with us through our worst days because He knows our hearts and understands how we feel. He is not the "Man Upstairs," far away and out of touch, but Immanuel—God with us, God among us, and God in us!

Is Jesus *your* Immanuel? Do you believe, have you accepted that He is your Savior and Lord? Not your grandma's, your parent's, or your pastor's, but yours? If so, do you believe, do you know He is always with you?

HE IS NOT THE "MAN UPSTAIRS," FAR AWAY AND OUT OF TOUCH, BUT IMMANUEL— GOD WITH US, GOD AMONG US, AND GOD IN US!

We allow the people we love the most to interrupt our lives. Our spouse can call us in the middle of a busy day and we will answer. Our kids can walk up to us with a simple need while we are in a deep conversation and we will stop to meet it. A dear friend can call at 3:00 a.m. and we will answer the phone to help.

When Jesus interrupts your life as He did the disciples' on the road to Emmaus or mine in the middle of a horrendous business trip, it will always be for our best and for the good of others. Accept His interruptions. Watch for His disruptions. Listen for His voice. Invite Him to enter your life anytime, anywhere, for whatever reason. When God shows up in power, you will truly discover what Peter called your "living hope."

Praise be to the God and Father of our Lord Jesus Christ! In his great mercy he has given us new birth into a living hope through the resurrection of Jesus Christ from the dead, and into an inheritance that can never perish, spoil or fade. This inheritance is kept in heaven for you, who through faith are shielded by God's power until the coming of the salvation that is ready to be revealed in the last time. In all this you greatly rejoice, though now for a little while you may have had to suffer grief in all kinds of trials. These have come so that the proven genuineness of your faith—of greater worth than gold, which perishes even though refined by fire—may result in praise, glory and honor when Jesus Christ is revealed. (1 Peter 1:3–7 NIV)

*Dear Lord,*

*Thank You for the interruptions that You bring into our lives. Right now, I want to give You permission to interrupt me. Forgive me for looking at Your movement in me as merely a distraction. Help me learn to see Your hand in everything. When I don't understand the detour on my path, give me the grace to trust that You are guiding and leading me through the rough roads and the storms, bringing me to exactly where You want me to be.*

*In Jesus' name, amen.*

# chapter eleven

# THROUGH OUR WORSHIP
# IN SPIRIT AND TRUTH

Years ago I boarded a plane in Calgary, Alberta, Canada. Arriving late as usual in those days, I soon realized there was only one seat left on the plane. On the aisle about halfway back, I sat down next to two women who were both wearing pink dresses and pink bonnets. What makes that little detail important to the story is that on that particular day I had decided to wear a pink shirt. I had a suspicion that many of the folks on the airplane thought I was probably the third member of some strange musical trio. Because it was so humorous and so obvious that we were dressed in matching outfits (although I didn't wear a bonnet that day), I began a conversation with them. We all laughed about our pink outfits.

During the flight, I found out they were conservative Christians who were on their way to a summer camp. Then one of the girls asked me what I did for a living. At that time I worked for Integrity Music and explained that the purpose of the company was producing modern worship music for the church. The look on the girl's face told me she thought she had hit some sort of spiritual jackpot. I was her captive audience. She reached into her purse and handed me a little booklet entitled *Instrumental Music in the Church—Right or Wrong?* You know when you see those kinds of questions in titles, the answer is always "wrong," right?

The pamphlet launched us into a long conversation of point and counterpoint. I laid out my premise for using instruments to praise God. She explained her beliefs for strictly voices being lifted to sing in the church with no accompaniment. I must admit that her argument made some sense. She had one valid point that when instruments are involved in a worship service, they are typically coming through a sound system that often makes it too loud for people to hear themselves singing, and therefore they don't participate. To her credit, I've actually seen that happen a lot.

Also, the music is often so overproduced in our churches that people watch rather than worship. The experience can feel more like attending a concert than being in a church service. As we were about to land in Salt Lake City, I took out my Bible and read to my pink-clad Christian sisters from 2 Chronicles 5:13–14:

> Indeed it came to pass, when the trumpeters and singers were as one, to make one sound to be heard in praising and thanking the LORD, and when they lifted up their voice with the trumpets and cymbals and instruments of music, and praised the LORD, saying: "For He is good, for His mercy endures forever," that the house, the house of the LORD, was filled with a cloud, so that the priests could not continue ministering because of the cloud; for the glory of the LORD filled the house of God.

When I finished reading the passage, I looked at them and asked, "Wouldn't you like that to happen in your church?" Their eyes got big under the brims of their bonnets. One of them looked at me and whispered an affirmative, "I think so."

## Facing the Music

In John 4, Jesus had His own lively discussion with a woman regarding worship. While the circumstances were quite different than mine, much like my exchange regarding the ladies' pamphlet, the subject matter certainly went deep quickly.

The woman had three strikes against her—she was a Samaritan, she was a woman, and she was of bad reputation in the community. But social, religious, and cultural barriers never stopped Christ from going to those whom everyone else considered to be untouchable.

"Sir," the woman said, "I can see that you are a prophet. Our ancestors worshiped on this mountain, but you Jews claim that the place where we must worship is in Jerusalem."

"Woman," Jesus replied, "believe me, a time is coming when you will worship the Father neither on this mountain nor in Jerusalem. You Samaritans worship what you do not know; we worship what we do know, for salvation is from the Jews. Yet a time is coming and has now come when the true worshipers will worship the Father in the Spirit and in truth, for they are the kind of worshipers the Father seeks. God is spirit, and his worshipers must worship in the Spirit and in truth." (John 4:19–24 NIV)

Jesus was clearly addressing the subject of worship and had every opportunity to talk about the importance of music. So why didn't He give us more direction in this art form that has become so crucial to today's church? I mean, after all, we often choose our churches based on the caliber of the worship team. We leave churches over the style of music changing. We gauge the spiritual success of a Sunday morning on how the music made us feel—or didn't. So this topic is obviously important to us. Why didn't Jesus even address this issue while He was on the subject?

But Christ gave no musical requirements at all. Why? Because evidently from Jesus' perspective worship doesn't equal music and music doesn't equal worship. He didn't talk about location but lifestyle—a 24/7/365 commitment. When we live for Christ and obey His calling, He seeks us out, and all that we do in His name can and will create worship to Him.

**WHEN WE LIVE FOR CHRIST AND OBEY HIS CALLING, HE SEEKS US OUT, AND ALL THAT WE DO IN HIS NAME CAN AND WILL CREATE WORSHIP TO HIM.**

Christ didn't place the responsibility of worship only on the leadership or those on the platform but on a singular credential: *a true worshiper who worships in spirit and truth*. Jesus said the Father doesn't just receive but *seeks* those worshipers. *Seek* means to go after. Therefore, God goes after those who worship in spirit and truth— Samaritan woman, Sadducee, sinner, or saint.

Jesus didn't tell the woman that she was nullified from this experience but simply told her the requirements. The essence of what He communicated to her was, "Look to Me because I am a true worshiper. I worship the Father in spirit and truth. And through Me, you can too."

Throughout the Gospels, Jesus first poured energy, time, and heavenly investment into twelve men; then second, into another close circle that included folks like Mary and Martha; and third, into all those He encountered as the Spirit led Him. He was moved with compassion to heal, preached the gospel of the kingdom, and dearly loved women and children, widows and orphans, the lost and lonely. Common sinners were drawn to Him and He hung out with a lot of questionable people. People just like you and me. And I'm so glad He did! We must make the unmistakable and undeniable connection to Jesus' daily investment into people and the kingdom to His words in John 4 as being a true worshiper.

## Passion, Pain, and Poetry

There is no question that in the United States, as well as in most first-world cultures around the globe, we glorify music. While music is a great common denominator, the rest of the world is more concerned with issues like being able to find food to eat and clean water. We often exalt mainstream singers and musicians to a higher level of humanity as a special brand of celebrity, right up there with television, movie, and sports stars. All we have to do is pull up any of the thousands of online videos of hysterical fans crying, shaking, and lifting their hands toward their artist of choice to see this dynamic at work.

During the past twenty-plus years, our churches have adopted this celebrity concept as well. Inside that paradigm, we have created our own genre of music and our own superstars. This was even a challenge for me during my time at Integrity Music. That is exactly how and why I can speak into this topic now on the other side. In too many cases, the need to "feed the machine" resulted in gospel songwriters trying to write the next Christian radio hit rather than creating a song to facilitate an encounter with the living God. Instead of the church representing the Creator by setting the standard for the arts, she began to follow the culture for artistic direction, reflecting more of the values in fallen mankind than in the new creation.

We have already established the fact that Jesus didn't broach the subject of music in John 4, so did Jesus *ever* mention music in His teaching? The answer? Never. Not one time. There is only one reference to music connected to Christ found in two of the Gospels:

> When they had sung a hymn, they went out to the Mount of Olives. (Matthew 26:30, Mark 14:26 NIV)

Yep, that's it. One verse. We have no way of knowing if Jesus and His disciples engaged in this type of worship at other times, simply because there is no other mention. Because of this one verse, we can assume that Jesus and His disciples sang, but the songs were not the priority or focus of their worship. He never gave us any instructions on what role music should play in worship.

Let's jump back to the Old Testament to the book of the Bible most commonly connected to music. Remember that the words of the psalms were originally set to melodies? Check out Psalm 69 and try to figure out a way to put a tune to this ditty by David, in case, like me, you aren't familiar with the tune of "Lilies."

**For the director of music. To the tune of "Lilies." Of David.**

Save me, O God,
    for the waters have come up to my neck.
I sink in the miry depths,
    where there is no foothold.
I have come into the deep waters;
    the floods engulf me.
I am worn out calling for help;
    my throat is parched.
My eyes fail,
    looking for my God.
Those who hate me without reason
    outnumber the hairs of my head;
many are my enemies without cause,
    those who seek to destroy me.

(PSALM 69:1–4 NIV)

*Those who hate me?! Many are my enemies?!* Can you imagine everyone at your church belting that one out next Sunday? Does acoustic piano or electric guitar suit those words best? Would a violin and a cello help soften the message? How many people would you lose, never to return after that song set? And I suppose quite a few people might not recognize that the words are indeed from Scripture.

Some of the psalms are beautiful pieces of poetry and we can easily see how the words can be sung in melody. My friend Chris Tomlin has certainly accomplished this skill very well and the global church has responded to his songs. Psalm 136:1–4 (NIV) is a great example:

> Give thanks to the LORD, for he is good.
> *His love endures forever.*
> Give thanks to the God of gods.
> *His love endures forever.*
> Give thanks to the Lord of lords:
> *His love endures forever.*
>
> to him who alone does great wonders,
> *His love endures forever.*

The inclusion of the book of Psalms in His Word proves to us that God is not afraid of our honesty. David poured out his heart to the Father, asking the hard questions, and God called him "a man after my own heart" (Acts 13:22). David said, "Keep me as the apple of Your eye: hide me under the shadow of Your wings" (Ps. 17:8). All the Psalms inspire and challenge us in our need for a healthy relationship with our Creator. That theme runs through this entire book of the Bible.

**GOD LOVES US UNCONDITIONALLY AND NOTHING WE DO CAN MAKE HIM LOVE US MORE OR LOVE US LESS.**

God loves us unconditionally and nothing we do can make Him love us more or love us less. When we attempt to hide our true feelings from Him, it's typically because we don't want Him to know how we really feel. As if He doesn't already know!

# The Noise of Your Songs

The following are words that, especially as a worship leader, I never want to hear God say:

"I hate, I despise your religious festivals;
> your assemblies are a stench to me.
Even though you bring me burnt offerings and grain offerings,
> I will not accept them.
Though you bring choice fellowship offerings,
> I will have no regard for them.
Away with the noise of your songs!
> I will not listen to the music of your harps.
But let justice roll on like a river,
> righteousness like a never-failing stream!"

(AMOS 5:21–24 NIV)

In most mainline evangelical churches today, the worship portion of a service is solely music and has been reduced to less than twenty minutes, even down to ten minutes in some cases. But often what has been diminished in focus has been made up for in enhanced production. Why take thirty minutes to "wow" a crowd when you can do it in fifteen? I appreciate great production and amazing pageantry as much as anyone, but people need God's presence *first and foremost*.

In the body of Christ, when we attempt to duplicate Las Vegas shows and mainstream concert tours, we unintentionally go full-tilt after the senses of the mind and body, while the only way a person can truly change is to go after their spirit by *the* Spirit. While so many are trying desperately to increase the number of people seated in the

WE CAN WORK VERY HARD TO CONNECT PEOPLE TO PROGRAMS WHEN WHAT THEY DESPERATELY NEED IS TO EXPERIENCE THE PERSON OF GOD.

sanctuary on Sunday, we must keep in mind that our mission is to grow disciples all seven days with the Sabbath being the time to rest and recharge spiritually at His throne of grace. We can work very hard to connect people to programs when what they desperately need is to experience the Person of God.

I know what it feels like when everything seems to come together in a worship service. The songs are spot-on. The keys in which we sing them feel good. God moves in a powerful way and everything just works. Afterward, you get the approving thumbs-up from the pastor. People come up and tell you how amazing they felt during the singing. But here is where the pressure begins. You know that somehow you need to replicate this experience next week due to the new expectations created by today's win. (I'm talking about job security here for the church staff.) That is how a formula is born and a template is created for the worship time.

So you look over the songs, keys, and tempos from last week's set list and try it all again. Duplicate last week exactly. But then when next Sunday comes and the pattern is repeated, this time *nothing happens*. No goose bumps. The people don't respond. The pastor just glares at you when you had anticipated a high-five. You wanted to force a response from the people, so it looked like and sounded like and felt like it did last week. But the set fell on its face, and God apparently chose not to listen.

The moral of the story is: we cannot finish in the flesh what God began in the Spirit.

One person who was instrumental in my life regarding the merger of ministry and worship was my pastor at Two Harbors Gospel Tabernacle, Ray Schaible. I had accepted Christ as my Savior at age twelve at that church. At the close of every service, Pastor Ray would invite anyone to come to the altar and pray as he strummed his guitar and worshiped the Lord. He not only gave me a love for God's presence, but also displayed an example of how to create an atmosphere of spirit and truth to give the Lord plenty of room to speak to His people.

**WE CANNOT FINISH IN THE FLESH WHAT GOD BEGAN IN THE SPIRIT.**

No production, no manipulation, no show, just getting out of God's way to make a way for His will to be done in hearts. That early influence is why I have always chosen to avoid the temptation to be an entertainer but rather to be very laidback about what I do onstage in leading worship. I prefer to be understated and what some may even think is underwhelming.

## The Splendor of His Holiness

One of my favorite passages in Scripture regarding worship that I often talk about and teach is found in 2 Chronicles 20. We are told that the people of Moab, Ammon, and Mount Seir were coming for King Jehoshaphat and God's people. Panicked, the king decided to ask the nation to fast and gather before the Lord. He stood in front of all Judah and Jerusalem, praying aloud to God, begging Him to save them. In verse 12 we read, "For we have no power to face this vast army that is attacking us. We do not know what to do, but our eyes are on you" (NIV).

Two very key points that are clear in these verses:

- Surrender (We have no power and do not know what to do.)
- Submission (Our eyes are on You, not on ourselves or the enemy.)

And therefore, God indeed responded to their surrender with His power and to their submission with His provision. The Spirit of God came upon Jahaziel, a Levite, and spoke:

> Thus says the LORD to you: "Do not be afraid nor dismayed because of this great multitude, for the battle is not yours, but God's. Tomorrow go down against them. They will surely come up by the Ascent of Ziz, and you will find them at the end of the brook before the Wilderness of Jeruel. You will not need to fight in this battle. Position yourselves, stand still and see the salvation of the LORD, who is with you, O Judah and Jerusalem!" Do not fear or be dismayed; tomorrow go out against them, for the LORD is with you. (2 Chronicles 20:15–17)

Jehoshaphat and the people responded by falling down with their faces to the ground before the Lord. Then some stood and began to worship "with a very loud voice." For clarity, let's recap the facts here:

- The people are about to be massacred by a massive army.
- They realize they cannot possibly defeat this lethal force.
- God tells them not to be afraid.
- God tells them to march against them but . . .
- God tells them not to fight, rather . . .
- God says to simply watch as He delivers them.

Here is the rest of the story.

> Now when they began to sing and to praise, the LORD set ambushes against the people of Ammon, Moab, and Mount Seir, who had come against Judah; and they were defeated. (2 Chronicles 20:22)

The key here is that the singers and musicians went out ahead of the army and led worship. The instruments and voices not only went *before* the weapons but *became* the weapons. The people sang, "For the Lord is good and His mercies endure forever," declaring God's goodness in a situation that was anything but good! Somehow, as only God could orchestrate, the enemy armies ended up destroying one another. The threat was over. God's people didn't have a single casualty and never even raised a sword. All they lifted were their voices and hearts in worship.

Our previous list contained what God did. But what did the people do in response? What actions did they take?

- They marched out to meet the enemy.
- They allowed the worship leaders to go out in front of the army.
- They worshiped instead of fighting.
- They experienced God's complete victory.

What can we learn from this passage regarding the spiritual realm? After all, even though we are not facing a physical battle, we are dealing with the same spiritual foe. What if we agreed that the ministry of the worship team is going out in front of the army of God's people to fight against the spiritual enemy of God and His people? How's

**CAN WE AGREE THAT WORSHIP IN THE CHURCH AND OUR LIVES TODAY IS NOT ABOUT THE RIGHT SET OF SONGS BUT THE PROPER BATTLE PLAN?**

that for a job description? How would such a change in focus and direction look in our church services? Could God's Spirit then be poured out on the body of Christ to experience His goodness and glory in a fresh and new way? Can we agree that worship in the church and our lives today is not about the right set of songs but the proper battle plan?

The intent of this chapter is simply to communicate that as tempting as it can be to take matters into our own hands when we desire to see God work, we cannot do God's work *without God*. He cannot be duplicated. His presence will never be replicated. His movement does not follow a formula. His activity has no template. We simply follow our heavenly Father's lead in life week in and week out, and then who He is in our lives will authentically connect to our worship.

We can and will experience the hope of heaven when God is both the catalyst and the center of our worship.

## Everywhere to All People

When our children were young, I found it nearly impossible to have any time alone for morning devotions or to play the piano just to worship by myself. No matter how early I got up, within a few minutes the youngest boys were at my feet, saying, "Daddy, play something fast! Daddy, we're hungry! Can you fix us some pancakes?"

I wanted to say, "Go wake up your mom. Can't you see I'm trying to have a devotional time?" But I always heard this still, small voice say, "Don, the best worship you can offer Me today is to fix pancakes for your boys."

And so as I poured batter on the griddle, I praised the Lord whom my family loved and served.

Whether I'm at home, on a stage in front of thousands, or in line at the grocery store, my life is always about something far bigger than lyrics and melodies. Ultimately, my days are about God working to reach people because everywhere I go, He is there and wants to work in and through me. The same is true for you! Far too often we've seen and heard about ministers displaying their Christianity only on the stage. I want my family and others to see the same guy at home off the stage as they see on the stage. Everywhere we go and everyone we touch is important to God.

Continuously in Scripture we see that worship begins with a state of the heart but then ends with some sort of physical response. When we share God's love and presence in practical, tangible ways, we worship. When we bring hope to the hurting, we worship. When we provide food, water, shelter, clothing, medical support, and education, we worship.

Humility and submission to God's plan appear to be the consistent catalytic factors regarding biblical worship, rather than

> WE CAN AND WILL EXPERIENCE THE HOPE OF HEAVEN WHEN GOD IS BOTH THE CATALYST AND THE CENTER OF OUR WORSHIP.

> EVERYWHERE WE GO AND EVERYONE WE TOUCH IS IMPORTANT TO GOD.

music. If our worship was more of a 24/7 lifestyle and our songs of praise then became the overflow of lives offered up to God, think how much more meaningful our singing would be!

If you agree to expand your definition of worship to include the daily activities of your life being given to God, returning His gifts back to Him in gratitude and honor, then no matter your past or your history, God does indeed have a calling *on* your life *for* your life.

Jesus embodied the Father's will *everywhere* to *all* people, and so must we. God cares just as much about a one-on-one encounter I have with a hurting person as He does an experience with thousands. Jesus fed the five thousand in public but He also healed the one in private, with both being equally miraculous. Therefore, the work we all do, as believers in His name, must be about the big picture of advancing God's kingdom on the earth. That is the biblical picture of worship.

> GOD CARES JUST AS MUCH ABOUT A ONE-ON-ONE ENCOUNTER I HAVE WITH A HURTING PERSON AS HE DOES AN EXPERIENCE WITH THOUSANDS.

Just like God has placed something in your hands as we discussed earlier, He has also placed something *in you* that is your vehicle to deliver His work to the people He wants you to reach. This truth makes any quality, gift, talent, or skill you may possess suddenly have a much larger purpose and goal than just your own success or satisfaction, or the approval of others. Everything you have been given is for a divine purpose and reason. He may provide you with different spiritual targets than mine, but He most definitely wants you to use your gifts to make a difference in a broken and hurting world.

When you give God back all He placed in you when He formed who you are, you are worshiping Him.

He gives and you give back.

You receive from Him and He receives back from you.

You are blessed and He is praised.

You are satisfied and He is glorified.

You worship and He is well pleased.

Our worship of God in spirit and truth is a vital aspect of experiencing hope, even in seemingly hopeless circumstances. I hope I have helped you think outside the box as we challenge ourselves to expand our definition of worship past the current culture in the evangelical church and broaden our boundaries to a biblical perspective. Without ever using a familiar hymn or chorus, you can offer worship and praise to God simply through your words.

Psalm 22:3 tells us that God is enthroned on the praises of His people. When we lift our voices in praise—with or without a song—we are building a throne for the King of kings and Lord of lords. The World English Bible says that God "inhabits" the praises of His people, and when God is with us, He will save those who are lost, heal the sick, deliver the oppressed or depressed, and provide for every need.

**OUR WORSHIP OF GOD IN SPIRIT AND TRUTH IS A VITAL ASPECT OF EXPERIENCING HOPE, EVEN IN SEEMINGLY HOPELESS CIRCUMSTANCES.**

# Keepin' It Real

At the close of a service in a small church in Florida where I had led worship, I was standing at the front of the stage to talk to people as I have always made a practice of doing. I looked up to see a couple walking down the aisle, headed straight for me. From the look of the man and his aggressive gait, I was not at all certain what I was about to encounter.

The man and woman were both dressed in leather vests, jeans, and biker boots with their arms covered with tattoos and various chains draped over them. Compared to the other folks in this congregation, they looked very out of place, really rough. As they walked up to me, the man barked out, "You!" He paused for effect as I waited for his next words, having no idea what to expect next. Then he continued, "I like what you do. You come across real. And my woman here—she likes it too."

The lady nodded in agreement.

Before I could respond with some sort of sheepish thank you, they turned on their heels and were out the door. I didn't see them again but I am confident they rode away on an old Harley, the man with "his woman" perched on the seat behind him.

The more I thought about that encounter, the more I realized the importance of the connection. The man didn't tell me what a great singer I was, or how incredibly I had played the piano. He made no comment on my talent. No. A much bigger picture was at play. The one I have tried to paint this entire chapter.

The man told me that I connected, I related to him, that something happened in his spirit. If from the piano what I had shared and sung reached into their souls, if I came across "real" so they could experience God, if they felt comfortable enough to come up to tell me, then that morning, we truly did worship. While music may have been the catalyst in that moment, God's Spirit made the connection to bring true hope to people's hearts.

That is worship—a very *real* encounter we experience beyond a shadow of a doubt because "the glory of the Lord filled the house of God."

Amen.

*chapter twelve*

# THROUGH HIS HOPE

When we lived in Tulsa and I had left Terry's ministry to launch out on my own, before connecting with Integrity, times were tough. We had two small children and I was constantly stressed about money. One day Laura looked at me and said, "Babe, you don't laugh anymore. You used to be so funny in college. What happened?"

I knew the answer to that question all too well, so I replied, "We have a house, two cars, two kids, and no steady work. *That's* not funny!"

Little by little, taking on one burden at a time, trying to be a good businessman, father, husband, provider, and Christian had changed me. Laura was right. I didn't laugh anymore. I had stopped joking. But the real root cause was that I had lost track of the reason for my hope by focusing entirely on the wrong things, focusing only on the negative of my circumstances. Yes, certainly, I still believed in God and knew that He loved me, but somehow I had lost sight of the fact that He was *still good*. I knew all His promises. I could quote you scriptures by heart all day. But allowing the hope of Christ to permeate my soul had gotten lost in the daily battles.

Today, the federal and state governments have declared our nation to be in an opioid crisis, meaning addiction to painkillers is at an all-time high across every economic and cultural boundary. Heroin is no longer just associated with the homeless addict but has become a closet drug of choice even among soccer moms in the suburbs. What could be driving this epidemic of trying to chemically kill our pain? My answer is that we are a nation that is losing hope. Or, maybe better said for many, a nation that has lost hope. Living without hope creates a mental, emotional, and spiritual ache in the soul that leads to a desperate desire to numb life at any cost.

> LIVING WITHOUT HOPE CREATES A MENTAL, EMOTIONAL, AND SPIRITUAL ACHE IN THE SOUL THAT LEADS TO A DESPERATE DESIRE TO NUMB LIFE AT ANY COST.

Hope is suffocating at the hands of our affluence and anxiety. We have even witnessed political campaigns run and won on the promise of hope, only to see, regardless of the party in power, no real and lasting change. As a result, we have become a cynical and distrusting people. The daily news brings us story after story underscoring hopelessness and heartache. In fact, I have chosen to limit how much mainstream news I watch or read. I have started viewing credible Christian news, because while still reporting the major news stories everyone covers, they will also showcase stories of healing, hope, and God's work in the world.

Part of the problem today is a misunderstanding of what hope actually is. We want it to mean that we will wake up one day and all our troubles will be magically over. We want a pill, a drug, a candidate, a device, or any fast fix, as in "I hope I can win the lottery this time." But that is the wrong definition *and* connotation. Objects can never offer hope.

Paul tells us clearly how we can experience authentic hope. His definition is not a campaign slogan or a catchy social media post merely promoting a better *tomorrow*, but a mission statement for a lifestyle committed to Christ and His kingdom *today*.

> Therefore, having been justified by faith, we have peace with God through our Lord Jesus Christ, through whom also we have access by faith into this grace in which we stand, and rejoice in *hope* of the glory of God. And not only that, but we also glory in tribulations, knowing that tribulation produces perseverance; and perseverance, character; and character, *hope*. Now *hope* does not disappoint, because the love of God has been poured out in our hearts by the Holy Spirit who was given to us. (Romans 5:1–5, emphasis added)

## Hope Before Faith

A close musician friend of mine who played trumpet and traveled with me in Living Sound, told me that he was going to go back to college when our tour ended so he could become either a brain surgeon or an eye surgeon. I laughed and responded sarcastically, "Sure you are, George!" After all, he was a musician like me! How smart could he be? Well, he did leave just as he said he would to go back to school—Ohio State University, to be exact.

As often happens among friends who take different paths, eventually we lost track of each other. But thirty years later, that all changed.

I was making an in-store appearance at Tower Records in Singapore. The manager handed me a business card and said, "A guy brought this by and wants you to call him." The front of the card read "George Bartley III, MD, Head of Opthamology at Mayo Clinic, Rochester, Minnesota."

Wow! George had done exactly what he said he would do and had obviously been successful. In fact, he is one of the top eye surgeons in the world today! I was very glad to be wrong about my musician friend from back in the day. He was visiting Singapore the same time I was and saw some of the publicity about my tour.

I called him and we reconnected over dinner in Singapore. George invited me to come to Rochester to visit him and even arranged for me to have a complete physical checkup at the Mayo Clinic.

When I walked in the front doors of the clinic, I quickly sensed one clear dynamic: *hope*. You could literally feel it. Hope was thick in the air and permeated the place.

There was a grand piano in the atrium that people were invited to play. There was evidence everywhere that the staff worked very hard to provide real answers for their patients' diseases and illnesses. Everyone spoke positively with great enthusiasm and focused on life, not death. In an environment where situations can so often appear to be hopeless, the Mayo Clinic was designed intentionally to emanate hope. You saw it, heard it, felt it, and sensed it, and most importantly, you believed there was hope.

I realized while talking with my friend George that *faith* is most definitely a religious word to people. But *hope*, on the other hand, is *not* religious. Hope is universal. Atheists, agnostics, Muslims, Buddhists, Hindus, along with all adherents of other religions and belief systems utilize the concept of hope. The object of faith is very different among the various religions, but hope has the common connotation that life can get better. People live their entire lives being relatively happy without faith, but life is difficult to survive without hope. We will perish with no hope, whether quickly or agonizingly.

But hope is the catalyst that can birth faith, the answer that drives faith. Hope is the belief that, in spite of what you see in the natural, God is supernaturally working in ways you cannot see.

A person who has hit rock bottom in life is a perfect candidate for faith, but I believe that hope is the spark in their spirit that triggers the thoughts:

> HOPE IS THE BELIEF THAT, IN SPITE OF WHAT YOU SEE IN THE NATURAL, GOD IS SUPERNATURALLY WORKING IN WAYS YOU CANNOT SEE.

*Is there a chance?*

*Is it possible that God loves me in spite of what I've done?*

*Is it possible that there really is a God who cares about me and has a purpose and plan for my life?*

"So then faith comes by hearing, and hearing by the word of God" (Rom. 10:17). When a sinner hears the message of the gospel, hope that God's Word is true becomes the spark that ignites faith. If faith is the engine, then hope is the fuel.

Hebrews 11:1 helps us connect faith and hope: "Now faith is the substance of things hoped for, the evidence of things not seen."

Hope comes from seeing a beautiful sunrise, a young couple madly in love, or a newborn baby, and believing that Someone is behind all

> **IF YOU CAN BELIEVE THAT GOD IS AT WORK IN YOUR LIFE REGARDLESS OF YOUR CURRENT CIRCUMSTANCES, YOU CAN MAKE IT THROUGH ANOTHER DAY.**

good things. All people want to believe that better days are coming. We can easily offer clichés to those walking through hard times, such as, "Hey, brother, hey, sister, just have faith." But it's very difficult to have faith when you have lost hope. If you can believe that God is at work in your life regardless of your current circumstances, you can make it through another day.

My friend Terry Law always said, "Hope is the confident expectation of the goodness of God."

## A New Song Out of an Old Place

One of the keys to the Christian life that I have discovered is that when we lose hope, when we can no longer laugh, when we feel robbed of our joy, that is exactly when we need to worship. "What?!" you ask.

I know! I get it! Allow me to explain. Those are times when we feel the least like worshiping. But that is exactly the best time and condition to seek God's face and His heart. The problem is, when we don't feel like worshiping, we don't. But that is when life usually gets worse. And then our hope will begin to decline even more. A vicious cycle can start a downward spiral.

In the musical *God with Us*, Jack Hayford and I wrote these words: "As deserving as God is of our worship and as much as He delights in our praises, He did not design this practice for His benefit. Worship is for our sake because worship is the atmosphere that welcomes His presence and gives place to His mighty works." Therefore, we do not praise God because we will get something. But when we choose to worship Him, His presence is welcomed and we are blessed.

> ## PRAISE PRINCIPLE #1
>
> When I choose to worship God, His
> presence is welcomed and I am blessed.

Throughout the pages of this book, I have continually communicated that my calling in life is to be a worshiper, not just a worship leader. Worship is in every facet of my life. Whether I am leading worship at an event, working with someone to write a worship song, involved in the production of an album, or hosting a radio show about worship, as a broken human being living in a fallen world, I don't always *feel* like voicing praise. But what I have found time and again is that when I don't feel like worshiping is actually the time I most need to do just that!

> ## PRAISE PRINCIPLE #2
>
> When I don't feel like worshiping is
> actually the time I most need to do just that!

You may ask, "Don, if my life is full of struggles and I am in the valley of the shadow of death, how in the world can I worship?" Or maybe the version of your question would be: "I was a strong, committed Christian until life pulled the rug out from under me—how in the world can I worship *once again*?"

How do you worship God when you've lost everything, you feel helpless, and your future seems hopeless? Your experience through the storm has caused you to rethink and question everything. Your heart is heavy. Your mind is reeling. Your spirit is dying. Whether you sang songs of praise just last year or haven't since you were a child, the words now seem empty and the melody that once soared in your heart has vanished.

How do you sing a *new song* when you still feel life is in an *old place*? How do you sing the Lord's song in a foreign land? The children of Israel asked that question:

> By the rivers of Babylon we sat and wept
> > when we remembered Zion.
> There on the poplars
> > we hung our harps,
> for there our captors asked us for songs,
> > our tormentors demanded songs of joy;
> > they said, "Sing us one of the songs of Zion!"
> How can we sing the songs of the LORD
> > while in a foreign land?
>
> (PSALM 137:1–4 NIV)

---

### PRAISE PRINCIPLE #3

I must sing a new song even when I still feel like life is in an old place.

---

Sometimes you have to look behind you to remember what God has done so you can begin to have faith for tomorrow. Think of the ways He has provided for you in the past. Remember what God has done for you and for your family. While your circumstances may have changed, His Word never will. He has promised to supply "all your need according to His riches in glory by Christ Jesus" (Phil. 4:19).

When God gives us a promise in His Word regarding salvation, provision, healing, and the like, we can stand firm on what He says because He will make it come to pass; maybe not in our timing, but in His.

When you receive a call from the bank about a lack of funds in your account or the doctor calls you with an unexpected negative report, you must make a conscious decision to worship God, not *for* the situation, but in the *midst* of the situation, even though you don't understand. You *choose* to offer what the prophet Jeremiah called "the sacrifice of praise." That's exactly why it's called a sacrifice.

Human understanding, pride, and self-reliance have to die when worship is chosen, even when you don't have a great reason and it makes no sense. You *choose* to bless God rather than *curse* your circumstances. Worship is making a choice to bless Him in the midst of a difficult situation. David said, "I will bless the LORD at *all* times" (Psalm 34:1, emphasis added).

## PRAISE PRINCIPLE #4

I *choose* to bless God rather than *curse* my circumstances.

# A Sacrifice of Praise and Thanksgiving

Therefore by Him let us continually offer the sacrifice of praise
to God, that is, the fruit of our lips, giving thanks to His name.
(Hebrews 13:15)

Thanksgiving is the first step on the journey into God's presence
when we thank Him for what He's done and then thank Him by faith
for what He's about to do.

> Enter into His gates with thanksgiving,
> And into His courts with praise.
> Be thankful to Him, and bless His name.
>
> (PSALM 100:4)

In light of the two passages above, think about what you listen to
on a regular basis. What plays in your house, car, work, and so on? Are
your choices creating an atmosphere of praise? If not, how would you
describe the atmosphere? What does your music speak or say to you? I
am certainly no legalist and I have nothing against clean mainstream
music, but as we mentioned earlier, praise confounds and confuses the
enemy in our lives. We must ask these questions of ourselves:

- What messages am I constantly feeding my spirit?
- What are those messages producing in my life?
- Is the music to which I am playing and singing along building
  a throne for the King of kings and Lord of lords?
- Is the music to which I am playing and singing along helping
  me grow in my relationship with Christ?

> ## PRAISE PRINCIPLE #5
> I will choose to continually offer the sacrifice of praise to God, and give thanks in all things.

Though the fig tree does not bud
    and there are no grapes on the vines,
though the olive crop fails
    and the fields produce no food,
though there are no sheep in the pen
    and no cattle in the stalls,
yet I will rejoice in the LORD,
    I will be joyful in God my Savior.

(HABAKKUK 3:17–18 NIV)

The key words here are "yet I will rejoice in the LORD." This is another choice we must face. When everything is going wrong, I will *choose* to rejoice in the Lord.

Do not sorrow, for the joy of the LORD is your strength. (Nehemiah 8:10)

But those who wait on the LORD
Shall renew their strength;
They shall mount up with wings like eagles,
They shall run and not be weary,
They shall walk and not faint.

(ISAIAH 40:31)

If you're feeling tired, worn out, ready to give up on life, why not try making the choice to rejoice in the Lord? See for yourself if these passages are true.

When Job lost everything, he said, "The LORD gave and the LORD has taken away; blessed be the name of the LORD" (Job 1:21). Again, he says, "Though He slay me, yet will I trust Him" (13:15), and he declares, "For I know that my Redeemer lives" (19:25).

Job had lost everything—his family, his fortune, and even his health. His wife told him to curse God and die while his friends ridiculed him and questioned his relationship with God. Job's state of being makes his words quite powerful and a stark reminder to us that our *position* has nothing to do with our choice to *praise*.

---

### PRAISE PRINCIPLE #6

My position has nothing to do with my choice to praise.

---

If you find yourself in a foreign land, fearful of what tomorrow may bring, look back and remember what God has done for you. Start with simple words of thanksgiving such as:

"Lord, thank You for Your Word and Your promise to provide all my needs."

"Thank You for the breath You have given me to offer You praise, even though I don't understand all that I'm going through."

"Thank You for the blessings that You *have given* me in my life, and now by faith, I thank You for all You *are going* to do."

As you begin to give thanks and praise in this simple way, you will begin to feel faith rise up in your heart, believing that God is able to take care of tomorrow and every concern you have. Keep your eyes focused on Him and not on the wind and the waves as your ship is being tossed about in the storm. He is with you there in your boat and you can trust Him! He can stand and say, "Peace, be still," whether to the waves around you or simply to your heart.

> ### PRAISE PRINCIPLE #7
> When I praise, faith will rise up in my heart, giving me the courage to believe that God can calm any storm I face.

## Fighting Fear with Faith

God knows the way you feel, and He knows the questions you have. In the middle of your pain and sorrow, your loneliness and fear, choose to trust Him, choose to bless Him, choose to lift a song of praise. At first, it may be very difficult because you are fighting all the questions with which you have been living for perhaps years, and there may be anger and bitterness in your heart toward God and others. That's okay. God knows and understands. He is in the middle of your darkest hour. He is there to help you, to guide you back to safe harbor. The sound of your praise and worship amid any hardship confuses and confounds the enemy attacking you.

> ### PRAISE PRINCIPLE #8
> The sound of my praise and worship amid my hardship confuses and confounds the enemy attacking me.

King David practiced this principle when everyone was against him and all seemed lost.

> When David and his men reached Ziklag, they found it destroyed by fire and their wives and sons and daughters taken captive. So David and his men wept aloud until they had no strength left to weep. David's two wives had been captured—Ahinoam of Jezreel and Abigail, the widow of Nabal of Carmel. David was greatly distressed because the men were talking of stoning him; each one was bitter in spirit because of his sons and daughters. But David found strength in the LORD his God. (1 Samuel 30:3–6 NIV)

The best weapon against the paralysis of fear is faith. Fear paralyzes us, but faith mobilizes us. The best way to engage your faith and restore hope is to worship, to find strength in the Lord your God.

---

### PRAISE PRINCIPLE #9

My praise will stop the fear that paralyzes me and mobilize my faith within me.

---

## Hope Can Flow from Our Mouths

A dynamic that exists in the confession of our praise to God is found in the power of our words, in the power of life and death in the tongue. We must be careful what comes out of our mouths, what we profess and confess, what we are speaking out about God and our own lives. Laura often says to me, "Babe, *listen* to your words." She is lovingly warning me to be cautious about what I am saying regarding God and my circumstances.

> A man's stomach shall be satisfied from the fruit of his mouth;
> From the produce of his lips he shall be filled.
>
> Death and life are in the power of the tongue,
> And those who love it will eat its fruit.
>
> (PROVERBS 18:20–21)

We must:

- Line up our mouths with our God
- Line up our words with the Word
- Allow God's Word to provide a balance to the problem at hand
- Recognize the reality of our situation doesn't have to be the finality for our lives
- Focus not on the power of our problem but on the passion of our praise

---

### PRAISE PRINCIPLE #10

Worship leads me to recognize that the reality of my situation doesn't have to be the finality for my life.

---

# Hope Flows Out of Generosity

In western culture, first-world Christianity, giving and generosity are often connected to the presumptuous promise of receiving God's blessings for a greater or even guaranteed level of comfort and security. This proclaimed prosperity from the Lord has become a sign of His blessing and favor.

While God certainly can and will bless our obedience to Him in giving, this cannot be made into a "give to get" guarantee. Teaching that God will give you security and comfort in exchange for your gifts is not at all a biblical pattern. Take any Bible hero from the Old or New Testament and look at the details of their story. You will be hard pressed to find comfort and security as a regular dynamic. Yet we see their lives in constant relationship with God amid their trials.

- Noah built a massive ark on dry ground with no rain in sight.
- Abraham packed up everything and everyone in his household with no idea where he was going.
- Joseph endured rejection and false accusation placing him in slavery and prison.
- The lives of all the prophets were constantly criticized and threatened.
- Moses and Aaron kept battling with Pharaoh day in and day out at the potential risk of losing their own lives.
- Hebrews 11 states that the disciples of the early church were tortured, falsely tried, whipped, stoned, sawed in two, and beheaded by the sword.

The biblical pattern is when you sacrifice, give, and obey, you will get more of God, not more treasure. In any discussion of worship through giving, we must begin by setting this cultural gospel straight by declaring the biblical truth. Scripture does encourage us to give the Lord our firstfruits—the first and the best part of our resources.

> "Bring all the tithes into the storehouse,
> That there may be food in My house,
> And try Me now in this,"
> Says the LORD of hosts,
> "If I will not open for you the windows of heaven
> And pour out for you such blessing
> That there will not be room enough to receive it."
>
> (MALACHI 3:10)

The one major question here that we must ask is, what exactly does God mean by "open for you the windows of heaven and pour out for you such blessing"? In western culture, we assume that means money, but does it? Heaven does not operate in the same currency as we do. God's ways are not our ways. What if God wants to give a heavenly blessing far greater than a larger bank account?

**SCRIPTURE DOES ENCOURAGE US TO GIVE THE LORD OUR FIRSTFRUITS— THE FIRST AND THE BEST PART OF OUR RESOURCES.**

The reason Jesus taught so much about giving and cautioned about wealth is because He knows that as sinners, the more we have, the more we realize what we have to lose. We don't want to sacrifice our best lamb. We would much prefer to raise the lamb ourselves and have more lambs. While God promised us daily bread, we want a pantry full of bread right now. An old Haitian proverb says, "A man is rich when he goes to bed knowing he has food for tomorrow."

True biblical generosity is giving away your future for the blessing of today. When we give, we open ourselves up to be vulnerable. But we also open ourselves up to be blessed.

Early in our marriage when Laura and I didn't have much of anything material, I will never forget hearing our pastor, Bob Yandian, at Grace Fellowship in Tulsa, teach on tithing and giving. Bob held up a twenty-dollar bill and said he was going to give the money to God. He then threw it up in the air toward heaven. As the bill floated back down to the stage, he said, "You know, folks, God doesn't need your twenty dollars. What He receives is the faith you give with your gift. If you have overcommitted yourself to the mortgage company, your car loan, or the credit card company, you have given your word that you are going to pay them, so as a Christian, keep your word."

I had never heard anybody else teach about giving in such a way. Typically, the topic of tithing is packaged in a big guilt trip that you must give 10 percent to God before you pay anyone else—*or else!* I had never heard before or since any pastor teach that if you give your word to pay back a loan, you need to do it, but even if you have to start giving to God with a nickel or a dollar, ask Him to receive your gift.

After that message, Laura and I agreed, "Okay, we're going to give ten dollars." We also prayed, "Lord, one day we want to give one hundred dollars like we gave You this ten. Then one day we want to give one thousand dollars like we give one hundred. Then ten thousand dollars like one thousand. Increase our faith, Lord."

Over time and obedience, God blessed each of our "one day" prayers and they were answered—the one-hundred-dollar day came, the one-thousand-dollar day came, and even the ten-thousand-dollar day came.

Through the years, we saw all those miraculous milestones occur. And, of course, to grow in giving those amounts of money, we had been blessed in our finances to be able to honor our original prayer. But what would have happened had we decided that first day when we heard Bob's teaching that we couldn't afford to give that first ten dollars?

Bob also taught, "When God gives the increase, don't eat your seed today that needs to be planted for tomorrow." For Laura and me, this teaching was a very freeing word and made us feel like we could do it. It gave us hope. There was no guilt involved. We were challenged to be generous and worship through giving. We started small, just as Bob had said. We then built up our generosity as God gave the increase. Being obedient to this practice took away the bondage we had felt for so long; the bondage into which we as Americans can so easily get stuck.

If you have never given of your resources, or maybe it has been a very long time, take Bob's advice as we did and simply start where you are. Worship God. Give of your money. Give of your time. Give of your energy. But give.

## Follow the Way Maker

In chapter 1, we talked in detail about Isaiah 43 and how God is continually doing a new thing in our lives. Practicing hope encourages us to stay focused not on *what was* but on *what will be*. Our hope brings the faith to step out into the new thing that God has for us.

Your focus need not be on *how* God will make a way, but on *who* makes the way. Keep your eyes on the *Way Maker*!

**KEEP YOUR EYES ON THE *WAY* *MAKER*!**

Before the song "God Will Make a Way" is sung in the musical *God with Us*, I say:

> With all the power inherent in His presence, it's still a fact that all of us face tough times, times a lot different than these moments of celebration. But tough times don't diminish the reality of His presence. Darkness will fall and clouds do gather; shadows will come. But our faith and our confidence in Him need never be shaken. And when we face difficult times and trials, He will be with us to make a way.

I want to return to the statements of hope and faith I first shared with you at the close of the introduction.

Do these words feel more real, more possible now?

Can you speak these out in faith over your life?

Do you believe God is able to bring these into reality for you?

Are you ready to pray these words daily, handing your life and circumstances over to the Way Maker?

*I can. . . . I can do this.*

*I will be able to overcome this.*

*I believe that will happen for me. I do.*

*What good is it to stop believing for something that can most certainly come?*

*I believe I know what to do. I know where to turn now.*

*I should make things easier on myself and give my circumstances to God.*

As we close, here is a prayer of renewal for God to place His hope into your story from this day forward for all eternity. If I was somehow able to sit down with you for a few minutes, this is what I would want us to agree in prayer together for your life. But the amazing thing is that through God's Holy Spirit, that can happen as you express these words to our heavenly Father.

*Dear Lord,*

*I choose to bless You. I choose to honor You. I choose to praise You, even though I don't understand all that I have been going through. I thank You for all You've done in my life, and by faith, I thank You for all You're about to do. With all my heart I declare that You are good and Your mercy endures forever. I choose to forgive all who have hurt me deliberately or unknowingly, and I ask that You begin to heal me, renew me, and realign me with Your will and Your ways, to make a way where there seems to be no way.*

*In Jesus' name, amen.*

# ACKNOWLEDGMENTS

As a songwriter, worship leader, and music producer I know it takes a lot of very talented people to produce a great music product, and throughout my career I've had the privilege of working with some of the best. The book world is completely new to me, but I quickly realized that without a lot of talented people at Emanate Books, HarperCollins Christian Publishing, helping me, *God Will Make a Way* would not have happened. Once again, I've had the privilege of working with some of the best.

Heartfelt thanks to Joel Kneedler for leading the team at Emanate Books and for believing in me and this manuscript. Thanks to my longtime friend Danny McGuffey at Iconic Media Brands for believing in this story and for delivering the first rough draft to Emanate. A huge thank you to Janene MacIvor, the senior editor on this project. You have worked tirelessly from the very first meeting, taking a personal interest in the message of this book, answering my emails within a minute any time of day or night, and making me sound a lot better than I am. It has been a joy to work with you!

Robert Noland, what a gift you are to me! I knew I needed help telling this story and the way you were able to capture my heart and my spirit after our first couple of meetings is nothing short of a miracle. Thank you for helping me find my voice in this book.

# ACKNOWLEDGMENTS

A million thanks to my manager, Jesse Sproul, and to all the staff at Don Moen Productions for your commitment to excellence in all you do. You are the best, and I am eternally grateful to each one of you!

To Laura, my precious wife, for standing by my side, loving me, supporting me, cheering me on, and always keeping it real! Someone once said, "There would never be a Don Moen without a Laura Moen." I know how true that statement is, because you complete me, and I love you!

Thanks to all our awesome kids—Melissa, Michael, Rachel, John, and James—for bringing such honor to me by living your lives in a way that is pleasing to God. I know He will always make a way for you!

To the Lord for blessing me with the ability to express my heart through melodies and lyrics, and now through this book. You have blessed me beyond what I could have ever imagined, and my heart is filled with thanks and praise for all You have done.

Finally, to all my friends who have prayed for me, supported me, and always encouraged me with your kind words, smiles, and hugs. I want you to know that whatever you may be going through today, God is working in ways you cannot see, and He will always make a way for you!

With much love and appreciation,
Don Moen

# NOTES

1. "God Will Make A Way" by Don Moen, (c)1990 Integrity's Hosanna! Music/ASCAP (adm worldwide at CapitolCMGPublishing.com, excluding the UK which is adm by Integrity Music, part of the David C Cook family) & Juniper Landing Music/ASCAP. Used by permission. All rights reserved.
2. Max Lucado, "The Master Weaver," Max Lucado, accessed June 6, 2018, https://maxlucado.com/listen/the-master-weaver-2/.
3. "Somebody's Praying For Me" by Don Moen, Claire Cloninger. © Juniper Landing Music (Admin By Copyrightsolver) / ASCAP, Don Moen Music (Admin By Music Services, Inc.).
4. Dr. James Young, "Mach Buster," Chuck Yeager, accessed March 7, 2018, http://www.chuckyeager.com/1945-1947-mach-buster.
5. "I Believe There Is More" by Don Moen, Claire Cloninger. © 2008 Integrity's Hosanna! Music (Admin By Capitol CMG Publishing) / ASCAP, Juniper Landing Music (Admin By Copyrightsolver).
6. John Wimber, "Quotes from John Wimber," Vineyard USA, accessed March 12, 2018, https://vineyardusa.org/library/quotes-from-john-wimber/.
7. "*Chariots of Fire* Quotes," International Movie Database, 1981, accessed March 25, 2018, https://www.imdb.com/title/tt0082158/quotes/?tab =qt&ref_=tt_trv_qu.
8. Bruce Wilkinson with David Kopp, *You Were Born for This: Seven Keys to a Life of Predictable Miracles* (Colorado Springs: Multnomah, 2011), 49.
9. "I Will Sing" by Don Moen, (c)2000 Integrity's Hosanna! Music/ASCAP (adm worldwide at CapitolCMGPublishing.com, excluding the UK which is adm by Integrity Music, part of the David C Cook family) & Juniper Landing Music/ASCAP. Used by permission. All rights reserved.

# ABOUT THE AUTHOR

A pioneer of the modern Praise and Worship movement, Don Moen has spent his career as a worship leader, producer, songwriter, and music executive. While a student at Oral Roberts University in the early '70s, Moen began touring with the musical group Living Sound and evangelist Terry Law. By 1986, Moen had recorded *Give Thanks* for the Hosanna! Music praise and worship series at Integrity Music, where he would serve as creative director, executive producer, and eventually, president of the label. During his tenure there, he sold more than 5 million units and signed worship leaders and songwriters, such as Paul Baloche, Ron Kenoly, Darlene Zschech, and many more. Today Moen lives in Nashville, Tennessee, with his wife, Laura, where he is president of Don Moen Productions and oversees his international nonprofit ministry, Worship in Action.

Facebook: www.facebook.com/DonMoenMusic
Instagram: @donmoen
Twitter: @donmoen
YouTube: www.youtube.com/donmoentv
Website: www.donmoen.com
Email: info@donmoen.com

Worship is more than the songs we sing. Worship is a lifestyle.

Don Moen founded Worship In Action in response to the great needs he encountered while traveling all over the world. It is his desire that our worship take place not only in churches or concert halls with our singing, but also in our backyards or around the world through our actions.

Through disaster relief, orphan care, and medical assistance, we exist to be the tangible hands and feet of Christ to people who have lost hope.

www.WorshipInAction.org